P. 40
P. 44
P. 46
P. 48 - What he
offered
to members.

Jesus and Jim Jones

JESUS
and
JIM JONES

by Steve Rose

The Pilgrim Press
New York City

Library of Congress Cataloging in Publication Data
Rose, Stephen C
  Jesus and Jim Jones.

  Bibliography: p. 228
  1. Jones, Jim, 1931-1978. 2. Peoples Temple.
3. Cults. I. Title.
BP605.P46R67   289.9[B]   79-17285
ISBN 0-8298-0379-3
ISBN 0-8298-0373-4 pbk.

The publisher wishes to express appreciation to the individuals and publishers
who granted permission to quote their materials. A list of acknowledgments
appears on pages 11-12.

The Pilgrim Press, 132 West 31 Street, New York, New York 10001

This book is dedicated to the memory
of all who died in Guyana
to all who mourn
to all who are left behind
and to all who try to understand

Contents

Preface

THIS IS A book about good and evil. It is about an event that epitomizes evil but that came out of many things that we call good. It is an index of the paradox of the event that the relationships between good and evil remain a mystery. I have merely tried to intuit its meaning for us at the edges of the mystery. This book is different from other books about Guyana because it starts with a different fact—the fact of God. The end at Jonestown was profoundly evil. To examine the experience is to be gripped by it, to gain a taste of its demonic essence.

Lois Rose, Caryl Johnston, Dan Darby, Irene Vassos, Walter Wink, Tom Boomershine, Fran Lippman, Bambi Neal, Paul Lippman, and many others knew I was writing about Jonestown and offered at various points tangible help, valuable insight, and simple support. Lois offered editing at the end. Caryl typed and rewrote and contributed some of her own ideas so that at some points the book is coauthored; fine by me.

This is a brief book. It can be read in an evening. The Appendix contains poignant letters and documents from a hopeful dream and an infinitely sad reality. The book closes with excerpts from a tape of the end. Throughout there is a cry to the institutions of religion not to separate themselves from Jonestown. It was a churchman who cried, "Die with dignity!" The demons won with a vengeance that will take much time to exorcize. Confronting *all* demons and deaths, however, is Jesus, who we believe and hope is victor over these powers. To be close to Jesus is not easy in our time. Yet it is to that struggle for closeness that this book is consecrated. It is through Jesus' victory that we are healed enough to remain here to celebrate the world that lies beyond control of demons, principalities, evil powers, and death's dreary shadow.

Steve Rose

Acknowledgments

Stephen C. Rose, *A Stranger Named Peace: Biblical Songs* (Persephone Music ASCAP, 1978). Reprinted by permission of Stephen C. Rose.

Stephen C. Rose, *New Rain: The Story of Jesus in Song* and *A Stranger Named Peace* (Persephone Music ASCAP, 1977-1978). Reprinted by permission of Stephen C. Rose.

Reprint of George Cornell article. Copyright 1978 by the Associated Press. Reprinted by permission of the Associated Press.

From *The Suicide Cult: The Story of the People's Temple Sect and the Massacre in Guyana* by Marshall Kilduff and Ron Javers. Copyright © 1978 by The San Francisco Chronicle. Reprinted by permission of Bantam Books, Inc. All rights reserved.

Excerpts from *Guyana Massacre* by Charles Krause. Copyright 1979 by Charles Krause. Reprinted by permission of Berkley Books.

Reprint of "Why Conservative Cults Are Growing" by Martin E. Marty. Copyright 1978 by Christian Century Foundation. Reprinted by permission from the December 6, 1978 issue of *The Christian Century*.

Reprint of documents from Christian Church Disciples of Christ. Reprinted with permission.

Excerpts from *Father Divine, Holy Husband* by Sara Drucker Harris and Harriet Crittenden. Copyright 1953 by Sara Drucker Harris and Harriet Crittenden. Reprinted by permission of Doubleday & Company, Inc.

Reprint of "Ex-Disciple Calls Cult 'Nightmare'" by Carolyn Pickering. Copyright 1977 by Indianapolis Star. Reprinted by permission of Carolyn Pickering Lautner and the publisher.

A Descent into Hell

Perchance he for whom the bell tolls may be so ill as that he knows not it tolls for him. . . . The church is catholic, universal, so are all her actions; all that she does belongs to all. When she baptizes a child, that action concerns me; for that child is thereby connected to that body . . . whereof I am a member. . . . No man is an island, entire of itself; every man is a piece of the continent, a part of the main. . . . Any man's death diminishes me because I am involved in mankind, and therefore never send to know for whom the bell tolls; it tolls for thee. . . . Another man may be sick too, and sick to death, and this affliction may lie in his bowels as gold in a mine and be of no use to him, but this bell that tells me of his affliction digs out and applies that gold to me, if by this consideration of another's danger I take my own into contemplation and so secure myself by making my recourse to my God, who is our only security.

—John Donne from *Meditation XVII*

On Thanksgiving week in 1978 the world watched in shock and horror an incredible mystery. An American white male minister was dead. So were most of his congregants. Over nine hundred people died: male and female, old and young, black and white.

The minister's name was James Warren Jones. The church was called People's Temple. He was a Disciples of Christ minister.

The deaths took place at the Temple's Agricultural Project at Jonestown, in the developing nation of Guyana. It followed the murders by Temple members of U.S. Congressman Leo J. Ryan, three American journalists, and a woman who tried to leave. A few months before, a former member had sworn under oath that this very congregation was indulging in a ritual that could be interpreted only as a threat of mass suicide. Now that had happened.

Were the deaths an act of faith or of brainwashing?

Were they acts of "revolutionary suicide"?

Was the whole thing the coerced annihilation of duped innocents? What, in God's name, had happened?

Some facts about the deaths will never be known. Others will take years to sort out.

This book does not purport to be the full story of James Jones or of the People's Temple. Nor is it an attempt to resolve the factual mysteries. Too many unanswered questions prevent a clear verdict on the degree of coercion within the cult; individual responsibilities at various stages; the influence of Marxism on Jones; the place of Father Divine, and many other factors. The rush of journalism, including three paperback books, immediately followed the Jonestown events and provided initial knowledge. But there needs to be corroboration of allegations at many points to arrive at something approaching a true picture.

This book is an introductory enquiry into some of the religious, ethical, and social implications of Jonestown. The John Donne quotation at the start of this introduction explains as well as anything the book's purpose.

James Jones was a Protestant minister. People's Temple was part of a mainstream American denomination. The Guyana commune belonged to the local council of churches. James Jones was at various times observed, defended, and praised by members of his own and other religious denominations. He received distinguished religious awards. To the end, he maintained religious

14

affiliations. He was part of the "continent" of the church.

Following the mass murder-suicide, Jones was viewed as a monster, a mad Eichmannlike figure. The bodies of the dead were deemed repulsive. This was partly an instinctive condemnation of murder and suicide. But it was also an effort to disaffiliate. The Disciples of Christ, Jones's denomination, spoke of instituting procedures for dropping autonomous congregations from their membership. The Vatican spoke of being for life, not death. Few voices echoed John Donne's conclusion that no one is an island, that any person's death diminishes others, that we may learn by seeing our connection to the death of another. Following Jonestown, People's Temple was no longer considered part of the *oikumene* (the universal church). Jones's body was to be burned, his ashes scattered at sea. People were relieved that he would not be given a place in a Richmond, Indiana cemetery, on home soil.

It was true that there had been a clear growth of a near Shakespearean madness in Jones. There had also been a willingness to allow murder, first of investigators and defectors, then of a whole congregation. Small children were to die first, a fulfillment of the madness, a compound of good and evil; guilt and pain; hostility and fear; an exercise in coercion with few historical precedents. There had been, before the event, monstrous acts of manipulation: suicide drills, where Temple members would drink a "lethal" beverage only to be told that they would be spared, that this was a test of loyalty to their pastor. And then finally there was the "real" suicide drill: a sip or injection of cyanide in a jungle camp that Jones called a "socialist agricultural commune." Perhaps the sanest thing would have been to rise up long before the end with a cry against the idolatry, against the madness. But some did. And few heard. And by the end, it was too late. Why, in the anguished words of one minister, did no one overturn the vat of poisoned fruit drink?

15

Yet even to the most reprehensible murderer at the time of death, a priest comes. Regardless of what James Jones became, he claimed membership in the church; and therefore he cannot be easily forgotten by others who are part of one religious community, or for that matter by the nation—even the world, which he so vehemently rejected.

So this is an essay about the self-annihilation of a fellowship. It is about a minister of the Disciples of Christ who was in good standing when a bullet went through his brain. It is about Jesus Christ, conqueror of death. And it is about us.

The debate after the Jonestown tragedy focused on one major issue, which is, When are we justified in abrogating assumed freedoms of religion (whether customary or Constitutional) to protect religious adherents from possible physical and mental harm? The government's immediate affirmation of the First Amendment in the Jonestown case was a praiseworthy effort to assure religious communities a certain continuing protection; or rather, noninterference. In practice, however, many feel that the evolution of the Jonestown disaster had much to do with government intervention. Some even argued that intervention *precipitated* the crisis. Others said that the government represented the last resort for People's Temple defectors, frightened by what they knew and desperate to save relatives from the fate they felt certain to be in store for them. How free from scrutiny should religion be?

Jonestown raises another question that is central to this essay: Is there a value system within the Judeo-Christian tradition that can be articulated? The answer is clear enough. That such a value system exists I have no doubt. Debate concerning morality over the past several decades has been characterized on the one hand by "situation ethics" and on the other hand by elaborations of "traditional positions." The trouble with situation ethics is

16

that there are few real situations that permit the luxury of the situational approach. In any given situation we act according to our position, our instincts, our inclinations (not the least of these is a desire to please "the group"). Thus it is important to clarify the fundamental thrust of biblical ethics to develop a basis for responding to events that happen too swiftly to allow extensive debate.

The earliest battle cry of the ancient Hebrew prophets is against all forms of idolatry. This includes allegiance to leaders who usurp the position of God, demanding worship of themselves. It also includes idolatry of bosses, groups, political movements, ethnic origins, class, race, party, or financial investment. The injunction against idolatry is the cornerstone of a biblical value system. Beyond this, biblical ethics propose:

1. Radical tolerance: the insistence that God is the judge—not we—of human mores and culture.
2. A transcendent obligation to the helpless: "As you did it unto the least, so you did it also to me."
3. Commitment to democratic processes: the implication of the coming of the Holy Spirit so that all humanity may participate in the re-forming of the world.

These positions interact dynamically. All point to the stratum of ethical consideration that underlies and emerges from biblical thought. They provide a possible foundation for an ecumenical consensus on values within the religious community. At least that is my contention in this essay.

Jonestown was a descent into hell. It was a hell of misplaced idealism, where death was made an idol. As we approach the year 2000, can we not anticipate an increase in the number of totalitarian movements drawing upon demonic, even satanic, energies?

Those with biblical roots must be as wise as serpents and

17

as gentle as doves; for somehow, amid all the evident corruptions of religion, it will be harder and harder to maintain the faith. Martin Buber concludes *I and Thou* with these words:

> Doom becomes more oppressive in every new eon, and its return more explosive. And the theophany moves ever closer, it comes ever closer to the sphere between beings—comes closer to the realm that hides in our midst—in the between. History is a mysterious approach to closeness. Every spiral of its path leads us into deeper corruption and at the same time into more fundamental return. But the God-side of the event whose world-side is called return is called redemption.*

This, drawn from Paul, is also relevant:

> Though we may speak with the tongues of angels
> Having no love we are nothing at all
> Though we may prophesy and dazzle with all knowing
> Having no love we are nothing at all
>
> There'll come a time when human tongues shall cease
> But love shall abide when the final veil shall fall
> We'll understand when we see face to face
> That without love we are nothing at all
>
> Though we should give what we have to the poor
> Having no love we are nothing at all
> Though we may offer our bodies to be burned
> Having no love we are nothing at all
>
> There'll come a time when human tongues shall cease
> But love shall abide when the final veil shall fall
> We'll understand when we see face to face
> That without love we are nothing at all.†

—Based on Paul's first letter
to the Corinthians, Chapter 13

*Martin Buber, tr. Walter Kaufman, *I and Thou* (New York: Charles Scribner's Sons, 1970), pp. 167-68.
†Stephen C. Rose, *A Stranger Named Peace: Biblical Songs* (Persephone Music ASCAP, 1978).

CHAPTER ONE

The Quest for Authority

It is possible to maintain that the People's Temple could never have arisen except in the context of a growing lack of religious authority in America. Authority is based on certain qualities worthy of admiration or devotion; wisdom, charity, compassion, courage, and fairness among them. In an ideal world there would be no need to distinguish between authority and power, but insofar as authority is lacking, power—coercion, the use of force of one sort or another—fills the void: systems of law, taxation, and government, which restrain a populace that would otherwise be an anarchic mass. The degree to which institutions of power embody the positive attributes of authority is the degree to which we have a civilization.

Today institutional power is considerable—whether in politics, the media, the military, education, business, labor, or religion. Yet there is scant institutional *authority*. Iconoclasm toward structures basic to civilization is widespread. Nor has American religion escaped this mood of disenchantment. Many good souls toil in the vineyards of faith, but the image of religion in general is low. Long before Jonestown the clergy were portrayed with cultural stereotypes such as Elmer Gantry: manipulative, hypocritical, and banal. There is today the cinematic version of the

19

minister as a bumbling officiant at weddings, unable even to remember the names of the participants, a comic figure. After Jonestown even clerical charisma and social concern may become suspect. Intellectually, biblical thought is deemed an anachronism by many, and few theologians have an impact beyond a shrinking constituency.

The political deception of this and the previous decade increased disaffection with prevailing institutions. We were left with a large reserve of alienated, vulnerable people in search of someone to trust. To answer the demand, there arose the self-appointed apostles of insular faith, who gladly feed upon human fear and superstition. Ten or fifteen years ago it would have been incredible for us to learn that a youngster would drop out of college and join a person like the Rev. Mr. Moon, reject family and friends, accept an arranged marriage, and affirm that the Korean millionaire is about the business of righting Adam and Eve's familial inadequacies. But today even philosophers and theologians applaud the sincerity of this movement.

Where does it come from, this intense longing to hear someone "speak with authority," this passionate need to know "the Truth" and to exclude everybody and everything that doesn't rigidly conform to it? And why do we elevate "sincerity" as a cardinal virtue when it is at once the mark of executioners and martyrs?

Today there is no clearer popular testimony to the church's loss of authority than its fundamental, embarrassingly visible and seemingly inevitable disunity. This is not merely institutional disunity but a lack of consensus on religious values as well, which has made organized religion a will-o'-the-wisp responding meekly to the ebb and flow of the culture. Amid a framework of greater religious unity, Jim Jones could not have avoided searching theological and personal contact with his peers. His congregation—especially because it made controversial claims about healing and other matters—would have been less able to escape thorough investigation. Nor is it likely that People's Temple would have been able to accumulate funds unilaterally or to move en masse to another country. It is a sad fact that there is so little unity and fellowship among America's congregations. Scant authority exists for questioning what takes place from church to church, whether it is a matter of theology or of human conduct. Churches tend to become islands unto themselves.

Religious unity is exceedingly difficult to achieve in a nation like the United States, where there has been a vigorous tradition of denominationalism. Within Protestantism alone there are more than two hundred groups competing for the allegiance of the religious seeker. Most of them purport to worship one who was killed, in part, for insisting that the temple be a house of prayer for all nations—a haven of unity. Is it any wonder that an outsider looks to the churches with some dismay? Each miniscule fragment, while it may appeal to this or that individual, also has less strength to resist social and economic pressures; for example, racism, or the class divisions to be seen in the various denominations. Yet today even the call to ecumenism seems to be a voice in the wilderness.

A. Alvarez has said of modern suicides, "Like sleepwalkers or those who were once possessed by devils, their life is elsewhere, their movements are controlled from some dark and unrecognized center. It is as though their real purpose were to find a proper excuse to take their own lives. So, however convincing the immediate causes, imaginary rewards and blind provocation of their final suicide, the act, successful or not, is fundamentally an attempt at exorcism."*

What was exorcised at Jonestown? The demons of the "fascist" society, which Jim Jones evidently hammered

*A. Alvarez, *The Savage God: A Study of Suicide* (New York: Random House, 1972).

home in his socialist perorations? How many believed it? Even Jones himself once professed a desire to return to American soil. The demons of Jonestown life? Clearly not, for while there was discontent, letters indicate that many of Jones's followers felt that they had chosen well. Exorcism of guilt? No small part of Jonestown life was guilt, and "dad" served as a reminder of it. But most striking in the Alvarez statement is the somnambulant aspect of the suicide event: the aspect of control from some invisible center, the suggestion of submission to principalities and powers. Whatever this power was that moved through Jones, most of his followers came to see it as indispensable—a power without which life was impossible. Part of this power derives from what I shall call the "Herculean conscience," an overwhelming desire to do good. It is the tragic side of our attempt to reconcile ourselves to a world pregnant with the possibility of nuclear holocaust and a battle to the death between rich and poor.

The term "Herculean conscience" defines the attitude of a small portion of the American populace, a group of people whose consciousness is formed by an existential awareness of major destructive forces in the world and by a strong desire to do something to combat them. The concerns of such individuals go far beyond the narrow pockets of self-interest to war and peace, ecological balance, racial justice, and human rights. The Herculean conscience is a product of social and historical forces and is quite different from the Freudian notion of a superego. It recoils at the inequities in the world and is battered by the constant rise in the media of apocalyptic data: oil spills, nuclear leaks, famine, torture, and reminders of individual madness. The development of a conscience that embraces these concerns seems a salutary event. It may hold the seeds of survival. But, as with all new birth, there is danger as well. For the Herculean conscience, allied with natural aggressive impulses, can give rise to a cast of personality dominated by a paranoia of the age.

22

The primary force behind the legitimate aspirations of conscience could be our religious institutions; both in their internal work of inspiration and education and in the willingness of persons touched by faith to proclaim courageously the basic values of elementary fairness, respect, and justice. Practical commitment of this sort would be an antidote to dead-end, desperate, paranoid movements and mentalities which submit, consciously or otherwise, to the forces of destruction.

It may seem bold to say it, but in many places in America the institutions of religion are contributing tangibly to this positive movement of conscience. In the wake of Jonestown, on the eve of a millennium, it is time for these institutions to link arms. It is time to reach across sterile divisions and work out a new consensus. It is time to alter the largely indifferent popular view of religion. The redemptive authority of biblical faith is tangible. A new expression of it—a massive renewal—is groping toward birth.

There is a basic argument to be made that Jim Jones was delusional, paranoid, self-destructive, and incipiently suicidal. The object of saying this is not to create a gulf between ourselves and Jones or between Jones and our time. Jim Jones was an exaggeration of a personality in an age whose signature is suicide. In a 1948 lecture (only recently made available in English), the French psychoanalyst Jacques Lacan sketched the metamorphoses of paranoia. He sees the modern ego as the "paranoic subject of scientific civilization." For Lacan, paranoia embraces

> the whole gamut of belligerent forms . . . rising in stages from a motivation based on the register of a highly primitive organicism (poison) to a magical one (evil spells), a telepathic one (influence), a lesional one (physical intrusion), an abusive one (a distortion of intention), a dispossessive one (appropriation of secrets), a profanatory one (violation of intimacy), a juridical one (prejudice), a persecutive one (spying and

23

intimidation), one involving prestige (defamation and attacks on one's honor), and revenge (damage and exploitation).*

An alternative to a paranoid world view lies in the movement toward seeing all things in the complexity of all their relationships. Gregory Bateson has done much to articulate an "ecology of mind" leading to desperately needed holistic thought processes. A study of Bateson is a good preparation for study of biblical faith, which at its root is holistic and nonidolatrous. Biblical faith is always actual, always historic, but never one-dimensional. The Herculean conscience to which I have referred is alien to it. There is no immediate biblical equivalent to its mighty appeals to "social justice"—sometimes heroic; sometimes pathetic; but almost always containing an element of "abstraction," which is foreign to biblical thought. It reminds us of the nature of a humanist who sometimes falls short in relationships with individuals.

Using Lacan's scheme, it is possible to consider some origins of the Herculean paranoid style in Jim Jones. Jim Jones the infant confronts a father who is functionally impotent and a punisher as well. There is an aggressive intention in the father, which will become part of Jones's later preaching. He will speak of beatings he received as a child. He seems to have carried a negative image of his father from the beginning. His father was always in the house; a victim of the First World War, he was unable to work. He was also a member of the Ku Klux Klan. Is there any other organization at once more impotent and more desirous of punishing? Shortly after Jonestown there was news of the beating of a black clergyman; this abomination was proudly claimed by the Klan. After Jones's death, the Guyana press printed a memorandum, allegedly in Jones's hand, sketching a crude Marxist faith and implying that the

*Jacques Lacan, *Ecrits: A Selection* (New York: W.W. Norton & Co., 1977), pp. 16-17.

24

1953 execution of Julius and Ethel Rosenberg caused him to think, even as a young man, of suicide as a protest against the world's injustices. During nearly three decades of ministry, Jones ran the whole gamut of aggressive paranoid reactions. He forged a grim dialectic of "them" and "us." If Lacan's construct is followed, the process of deterioration seems an almost circular motion. The end is poison (Lacan's beginning point). To each of Lacan's paranoid negations can be added an aspect of Jones's Herculean conscience, making a macabre marriage indeed:

1. "A highly primitive organicism" (poison)—*Revolutionary suicide.*
2. Magic and evil spells—*Heightened intuitive capacities; claims of mind reading.*
3. Telepathy, influence—*Attempts to control criticism in the name of resistance to persecution.*
4. Lesion, physical intrusion—*Necessity of fusing followers into a "redeemed community" via sexual relations, sadism.*
5. Abusiveness, distortion of intentions—*"Catharsis" sessions, punishment as "redemption."*
6. Dispossession, appropriation of secrets—*Omniscience, clandestine investigations, "confessions."*
7. Profanation, violation of intimacy—*Breaking of natural family ties.*
8. Prejudice—*Assumption of persecution by "enemies."*
9. Persecution, spying, intimidation—*All three of these.*
10. Concern with prestige, with one's honor—*Self-comparison with "other martyrs," such as Dr. King. Concern for "my place in history." Preoccupation with the end.*
11. Revenge, damage, exploitation—*The ultimate aggression: "revolutionary suicide," poison.*

The circle is complete. Hardly exact, but suggestive.*

*Consider, for comparative purposes, aspects of the Johnson and Nixon administrations.

25

Modern drugs . . . have . . . made suicide more or less painless, they have also made it seem magical. . . . Dostoevski's Kirilov said that there are only two reasons why we do not all kill ourselves; pain, and the fear of the next world. We seem, more or less, to have gotten rid of both. In suicide, as in most other areas of activity, there has been a technological breakthrough which has made a cheap and relatively painless death democratically available to everyone. Perhaps this is why the subject now seems so central and demanding, why even governments spend a little money on finding its causes and possible means of prevention. We already have suicidology; all we mercifully lack, for the moment, is a thoroughgoing philosophical rationale for the act itself. No doubt it will come. But perhaps that is only as it should be in a period in which global suicide by nuclear warfare is a permanent possibility.*

So says A. Alvarez, the author of the best modern treatment of the subject.

Nuclear war is but one of the possibilities that engages the Herculean conscience. Suicide becomes not merely a way of opting *out* of history but of playing a part *in* history. And, the truth is, the act has at times made a difference. The threat of self-destruction in an age of mass media becomes one significant way that the atomized individual can gain a world audience for a brief instant. Recall the self-immolations of Vietnam. Jones tried to make *his* deaths painless, another modern notion. But he did not succeed. There was too much screaming. People were not "dying with dignity." He laced the cyanide with Valium; this is in accord with Alvarez' projection. It was a nearly exact fulfillment of Dostoevski's worst predictions for a nonbelieving world. The nomenclature of God was cast aside, and what remained was the rhetoric of the socialist revolutionary. "If God is dead, anything is possible." It may be that when God dies, we die too. (Organized

*Alvarez, op. cit.

religion, by "finalizing" God by identifying "him" with membership in the institution, contributes inadvertently to this cultural loss of the reality of a Holy One in our midst and beyond us.)

To speak of Jones as an exaggeration in an age whose signature is suicide is not to picture Guyana as the end of civilization. It is only to point out a tendency, a possible breaking point, to warn against it. It is to ask the reader to think about the implications of a world where there is a vast power in an individual or group to follow destructive impulses of a God-denying nature. Insofar as religion merely takes *from* the world, refusing to offer its own resources—historic and revelatory—the truths that can release conscience from its Herculean fixations and thereby exorcise paranoia, by naming and accepting the reality of aggression, will remain hidden. The Herculean conscience will have its day. It will envelop the world in its own dialectic of suicide. This is the reason the solution to the mystery and tragedy of Jonestown must be seen as lying within the realm of faith.

The logic of Jonestown exists in some form wherever minds are gripped by "spells," catchwords, stereotypes, and substitutes for thought: abusive politics, prejudice, intimidation, spying, and lust for prestige. There arises an inevitable confusion between power, which is incursion; and authority, which is moral character. We are even tempted to cry out for more "law and order," more state, more bureaucracy to "protect" ourselves. But I think the answer lies not in fearful retreat but in discovering an authority that cannot be moved. *The most pertinent sign of redemption is possession of an internal authority that needs no power whatsoever to reinforce it.* Jonestown shows that the answer to the challenge before us does not lie in a rejection of religious faith but in rediscovering faith's capacity to grapple with the tenacious forces of sin and evil that have hardly been eradicated by our modernity. The holistic

27

world of biblical perception is a bright streaming-in of light from many dimensions; painful, perhaps, for eyes more accustomed to the thought of one dimension only. Yet Jesus is there in the center of it and, too, in the center of our faith, despite all of our tragic dividedness. When other authorities fail or exceed their limits, becoming oppressive powers—when the state, science, the humanities, custom, tradition, ideologies, and systems crumble amid the tremors of history—it is to the prophetic tradition and, above all, to Jesus that we turn.

The Herculean conscience is an understandable phenomenon in a world that has crossed a threshold of moral evolution. People have become aware of oppressive, inhumane conditions; and they are aware, too, of the emptiness and banality of evil, to the extent that the *evil conditions themselves are a source of psychic as well as physical oppression.* Perhaps someday it will be understood that the new twentieth-century media had a role to play in this by heightening our conscience and troubling our awareness. A conscience sensitive to evil and exposed to the self's own aggressive impulses can all too easily lapse into suicidal paranoia. The sweep toward death is very close. Thus the stakes of faith are incomparably high. A conscience healed by biblical insight and faith can live on in this world, with patience and self-acceptance, and in hope of being a vehicle for changing it for the better.

CHAPTER TWO

Evidence

Shortly before the end Jim Jones wrote from Guyana:

The warm, gentle trade winds have come up and the glow of
the evening is subsiding quickly into the clear, star-filled night.
There is such peace here. There can't be anything so fulfilling
anywhere as living this communal life. We watered the garden
today. We grouped into bucket brigades to haul water to a
two-and-a-half-acre plot where we are experimenting with a
North American crop. We sang and laughed and joked the
whole time, and in the spirit of joy in our accomplishment,
urged each other on to a faster pace. We had the whole job
done in two hours. I love to work. I was at the beginning of the
line, bringing spring water up out of the well that brims full no
matter how much we take from it. One who leads is also one
who works. And working together this way, we are making
the land produce faster than we can clear it.

I work in the field whenever I can—whenever I am not
helping coordinate the defense against the attacks on us in the
United States. It strikes me as immensely sad that the vast
majority of people submit to the regimentation and extreme
tension of a highly technological society. They pay such a high
price in strokes, hypertension, physical diseases and mental
stress. And yet those who dare to live for high ideals rather
than the mediocrity, apathy and indifference that are the order
of the day, become the objects of vindictive harassment.

Cooperative living provides such security. It provides the
structure to see that everyone's needs are met. It maximizes

29

everyone's own individual creativity and allows time for pursuit of individual interests. We have classes in rugmaking, weaving, tanning hide, canning, and myriad academic subjects. Seniors and youth alike are learning every type of craft, carpentry, welding, electrical work and even medicine. We have the best nutrition and a very high level of preventive medicine. Each resident has a blood pressure and TPR test (temperature, pulse and respiration) once a week.

We enjoy every type of organized sport and recreational games. Musical talents and arts are flourishing. We share every joy and every need. Our lives are secure and rich with variety and growth and expanding knowledge.

What kind of security can money buy to compare to this? I cannot help thinking about some like Howard Hughes—one of the richest men in the world who died of neglect and lack of proper medical attention. Or John Paul Getty, a billionaire who refused to pay a ransom for his own grandson and kept pay phones in his mansions. When we had a nursing home years ago in the Midwest, a well-to-do gentleman was on his deathbed; his relatives started fighting over his handkerchief and bedside belongings the minute he lost consciousness. I was sure the failing man was hearing them bicker. A nursing assistant who was present at the time, Mary Tschetter, had to ask them to leave the room. Carrie Langston, a member of our church, worked for years taking care of very wealthy people, and said that sometimes even before they passed, their families came in and stripped their homes of all their possessions.

Here, even though we are under the financial burden of developing this agricultural project, we paid for cosmetic surgery for one of our members whose appearance was marred from birth. We could hardly afford to do this, but her psychological development was being hampered, and to us, human values are more important than material things. Surely living for oneself, amassing individual wealth or fighting to stay on top of the pack is no way to live. Your personality and your worth become defined by what you own rather than by what you are or can do for others. When you are without ideals, you live alone and die rejected.

We have got to find a way to share the wealth of the world more equitably. It seems unless America learns this, she will meet as tormented an end as the multimillionaires she has spawned. In a very real sense, we came here to avoid contributing to the destruction which the country of our birth continues to inflict on less prosperous nations. How can one live free of guilt when one's resources go to sponsor the kind of atrocity I read about that took place in Rhodesia? A child was forced to beat his own father, a Black African leader, on the privates until they were severed from his body. The father died from the beating. Several of the persons directing the atrocity were members of the U.S. military, one of them a major. How can individual Americans consider themselves blameless when their money, through agencies like the International Monetary Fund, is used to destabilize popularly elected governments such as in Portugal? Just America's past sins alone should cause one to feel guilt. Here we have the clean feeling that we are not contributing to this kind of abuse of power. Perhaps people of conscience in America can challenge such policies privately, but how can you avoid the feeling that you're compromising what you stand for?

I will be back one day. But just as others who have been courageous enough to stand up and speak their minds in America have paid the final price—whether revolutionary as the first Americans who believed in liberty or death, or whether nonviolent, like Martin Luther King—I also expect to die for my beliefs. And in these days you don't have to be as great a man as Martin Luther King to die for taking a stand.

For all those who would be concerned about our eventual fate, you should know we have found fulfillment. We have gotten ourselves together. We share every moment. When I see the seniors happy and productive, when I see the children gather to perform a play, I know we have lived. Life without principle is devoid of meaning. We have tasted life based on principle and now have no desire to ever live otherwise again. You do not know what happiness is until you have lived up to your highest. You should come. Often I wish I could be there with you, but I had no choice. They were going to harm youngsters and seniors, and I am a leader who could not leave one soul who looks to me for guidance to that fate. I feel it is my duty to protect them from senseless destruction. We were being set up by provocateurs. I am not about to let us be used as an excuse to bring hardship down on the people of the United States.

Now there is peace. For the seniors there is freedom from loneliness and the agony of racism. For the children, as simple a relief as no more bedwetting or bad dreams. We have found security and fulfillment in collectivism, and we can help build a peaceful agricultural nation.

I know some of you there will suffer for the ideas you now guard carefully behind closed doors. One civil rights leader has called to tell us the same writers who were after us have come around to check on him. But when you have stood up for your rights, when you have done all you can for oppressed people, there is no longer any fear. I know well that I am not as articulate as Martin Luther King, Jr., Malcolm X, or Eugene V. Debs, but my head is on straight and I am well trained for battle. No one could be more fearless or principled. Neither my colleagues nor I are any longer caught up in the opiate of religion nor the narcissistic indulgences of trying to keep ourselves young. And yet, in the balmy tropical sun and gentle breezes, we have shed the physical afflictions of the dog-eat-dog world. Arthritis, diabetes, kidney ailments, hypertension—they have been reduced to almost nothing here.

We have found a healthy and meaningful existence. There are high relationships here, ones that do not come just out of sex, but by sharing and living the highest ideals. We have passed beyond alienation and have found a way of living that nurtures trust—one that could speak to a society grown cynical and cold.

● ● ● ●

It is obvious someone or some group wants to denigrate what is going on here. A long time ago a high-ranking official had told us we would be having difficulty in the future. We did not pay much attention at the time, but now it all fits together like pieces to a puzzle. A powerful agency he had mentioned was, as crazy as it sounds, threatened because we're too effective at organizing people of all races to work together. In the eventuality of economic crisis, it was thought we would have too much organizing potential among the economically deprived of all races. Organization for survival of the poor was not on their agenda.

He told us also that there were individuals planted in our ranks who would try to promote terrorist activities. When this fact happened, we were reluctant to credit their motives to deceit, and we regarded them as ignorant and youthful fanatics. But now, when we see these same ones who tried to steer us on a violent course being picked up and dignified by some of the media—with no thought given to challenging their word with as much as a lie detector test—it is obvious that the official's warning was correct. We had provocateurs in our midst.

There have been so many obstructions thrown in our way throughout the years. We had thought several years ago to do a documentary film about our work in alternatives to drug addiction, antisocial behavior, and violence. The next morning, after having discussed our ideas over the telephone, we received a phone call from an "agent" for some "movie producer" offering a face-to-face meeting for a promising contract. When we checked through the police to locate the source of the call, we found an office building with no such company where someone could have easily been waylaid in a corridor. It is difficult to convey this kind of intrigue that has followed us in a few short lines—there have been more death threats and attempted frame-ups than I can begin to count, not only on me and my family, but also on many of the church leaders.

Even if the powerful were to succeed in smearing and destroying this one voice for racial and economic justice, it is ridiculous that they underestimate the intelligence of the general public, the little man I have represented who had no voice. Someone will always rise up to speak again. People are beginning to see through the overkill that has been perpetrated against civil rights leaders, and I believe the people will prevail.

Thus Jim Jones. Can there be a more moving and clear expression of the wedding of Herculean conscience with the paranoia of the age?

No event in recent history has pressed journalists to prepare a story more hastily than Jonestown. The People's Temple and Jim Jones had been investigated as early as 1972. But the sum total of what was known was small, and there was a great desire on the part of many people to learn more. Many people I talked to after Jonestown told me that for several weeks they could think of little else.

There is another aspect of journalism that every reporter knows: the importance of maintaining a story's flow. Doing this can sometimes involve using quotes without attribution, giving credence to dubious witnesses, and relying on other published stories without checking substantive allegations. High journalistic standards are necessary to resist the temptation to distort or stretch evidence.

There are several sources of evidence about Jonestown. First, there is direct observation by journalists and other outsiders. This kind of information is rare; its reliability is never fully assured. (I have included examples in the appendix. Many of these paint a highly positive picture of People's Temple activities.)

There is a second kind of evidence. This is the testimony of former members, sometimes called defectors. For Jonestown, this record is the major source of criticism and negative allegations. Among such testimony, affidavits presented to the court on penalty of perjury are probably the most reliable.

Examples of various evidence must be read not as final proof but in terms of the relative biases of the various witnesses. Here is a brief sampler, designed to provide some basis for judgments about Jonestown.

1. The San Francisco Temple: A Healing Service

Marshall Kilduff of the San Francisco *Chronicle* described a People's Temple service that he attended in January 1977. He says he entered the Temple accompanied by aides, walking through several doors with locks and alarms. Aides explained this by mentioning threats to Jim Jones, letters from Nazis, and other reasons. To Kilduff, the Temple seemed "a bustling showplace of self-help and charity." Child-care facilities; a medical room; an audiovisual center, complete with ham radio station for communication to Guyana; a printshop; and living areas were noted. Kilduff was taken to the main auditorium where he then sat in front with aides on all sides. He estimated a crowd of 1,500-2,000 persons, three fourths of them elderly blacks. The balcony was filled with young people.

Jones's sermon began with questions and answers. A man asked him what Jesus was like. "He threw the moneychangers out of the temple," Jones replied. Another man, with a bad back, complained. "Give him a hug; show him that divine love!" cried Jones to a woman who had already testified to Jones's healing power. She did. "It's gone! The pain is gone!" the man cried "Thank you, Jim! I'm all well!"* Kilduff does not say whether he believed the cure was genuine or not.

2. Charles Krause on Jonestown

Charles Krause, of the *Washington Post*, survived the airport shootings in Guyana and wrote:

> As a reporter I wonder now if I was terribly naive at Jonestown. Did I ignore evidence that Jonestown was closer to what the Concerned Relatives (name of a group of former temple members who urged investigation by Congressman Leo Ryan)

*Marshall Kilduff and Ron Javers, *Suicide Cult* (New York, 1978), pp. 5-7.

said it was: a concentration camp run by a madman—than a tropical paradise Jones and the others claimed? Even now, I am not convinced that the majority of people there wanted to leave, no matter what the reality of Jonestown.*

In general, Krause's comments on the commune were favorable. "I was convinced that Jones was very sick, both physically and mentally. But the People's Temple hadn't struck me as a crazy fringe cult. . . . It seemed to me that the People's Temple had a legitimate purpose, a noble purpose, and was more or less succeeding."

Krause recorded several of Jones's remarks as the end drew near. "He had told us he might have cancer, that he had lost 31 pounds in recent months, that his temperature had reached 103 degrees on that day (November 17) and that 'in many ways I feel like I'm dying. I've never felt like this before. Who the hell knows what stress can do?'"

Krause also reported Jones's statement about his "son" John, object of a custody suit by former Temple members Timothy and Grace Stoen.

> He said that he, not Tim Stoen, was the father of the child. "He's my son, he's my son." I asked him if it would be correct to say that he had an affair with Grace Stoen. He said: "I never had an affair with anyone but my wife." But he also said Tim Stoen asked him to have sexual relations with Grace. "I needed him (Stoen) in the church at the time," Jones said. "He asked me to do it, and I did it." (This relationship with Grace continued for four years.) "I stayed with her until she asked me to marry her. . . . She's a manipulative, destructive female. I would not like to hurt her, but I know whose child it is. . . . I can't give up the child. Oh, God, it's so painful. . . . I feel so guilty about it."†

Concerning defectors, Jones told Krause,

Threat, threat, threat of extinction. I wish at times I wasn't

*Charles Krause, *Guyana Massacre* (New York, 1978), *passim*.
†Ibid.

36

born. I understand hate; love and hate are very close. They can have me. . . . I do not believe in violence. Violence corrupts. And then they say I want power. What kind of power do I have, walking down the path talking to my little old seniors (elderly residents)? I hate power. I hate money. The thing I want now is never to have been born. All I want is peace. I'm not worried about my image. If we could just stop it. But if we don't, I don't know what's going to happen to 1,200 lives here.*

The investigating party arrived at Jonestown on November 17. Krause reports that an angry Jones refused his wife's suggestion that the party be lodged at Jonestown for the night. "It's a mistake. I don't want them here."

Of his first impressions, Krause wrote, "It seemed so peaceful, so orderly, so bucolic. . . . I noticed immediately that contrary to what the Concerned Relatives had told us that everyone seemed to be quite healthy. . . . The Jonestown people seemed quite hospitable. I couldn't understand why there had been such a fuss; the buildings were impressive; . . . the people seemed healthy, rational, friendly."

The next day, Krause rode to what was to be an ambush at the Kaituma airstrip. "No one, not even the defectors on our truck, had offered any proof that the 900 or so people at Jonestown were being starved, mistreated, or held against their will."

3. Ron Javers on Jonestown

Ron Javers was the *San Francisco Chronicle* reporter on the scene. He was far less sympathetic than Krause. Jones responded to photographic evidence that one girl had been beaten. Jones said, "We don't use physical punishment anymore. We stopped it a few months ago—maybe a year.

*Ibid.

The girl got seventy-five spankings because her mother, Mrs. Mertle, began it herself. The girl was a kleptomaniac. Her mother demanded that punishment. I said to her mother, 'You spank me first.' I often took spankings."*

Jones admitted to Javers that there had been "catharsis sessions" where physical and psychological abuse was aimed at members. "We had it," he said, "but not anymore."

Jones first denied the presence of guns at the commune, but, pressed, admitted it. "Guns, yes. But how many, I don't know."

To the assembled journalists he said, "I have doubts you can print the truth. If you printed the truth, you'd be in trouble. The press has an open season on anybody who has any kind of adversary life-style."

To questions about sex in Jonestown, he replied, "No sex? Bullshit. Bullshit. Bullshit. Thirty babies have been born since the summer of 1977 in Jonestown."

"Obviously there is a conspiracy," said Jones. Javers asked who was in the conspiracy.

Who conspired to kill Martin Luther King, John F. Kennedy, and Malcolm X? Every agency in the U.S. government has given me a hard time. I have tried to build a community that is an alternative to the culture of the U.S. I took street addicts and dope pushers and brought them here and I have been successful. Whoever is conspiring to destroy the People's Temple is foolish. It's foolish to destroy voluntary socialist society. Why would anyone be afraid of me? People are killing me with that kind of rubbish.†

I have found no account of any reporter asking Jones about suicide drills, even though this serious fact had been charged prior to Jonestown.

*Kilduff and Javers, op. cit., p. 84.
†Kilduff and Javers, op. cit., pp. 161-66.

4. Accounts of the End

Accounts of the actual events following the airstrip massacre on November 18 were limited initially to the testimony of a few eyewitnesses. Most journalistic accounts were based on talks with Odell Rhodes, Jr., who claimed he was present. The *National Enquirer* purchased from Rhodes an exclusive "eyewitness account" in which Rhodes spoke of holding children he loved while they died and of witnessing two nurses force poison down the throat of Julie Reynolds, "a sweet, adorable twelve-year-old." "Two or three times they did it and each time Julie spat it out. Then they killed her. She died a sickening death."*

Another witness-survivor was Stanley Clayton. "Nurses took babies right out of their mothers' arms. Mothers were frozen with shock, scared out of their wits. A lot of people were crying and screaming at the fact that babies were dying. Jones began shouting at one mother, then at the others, "Shut up, shut up. Stop your crying. Die with dignity."

Rhodes's account included the story of Christine Miller, who spoke out against suicide and pleaded openly for the commune's 260 children. According to Rhodes, Jones became furious, and the crowd coalesced against the woman. "Jones told her that with him dead, no one would be happy." The crowd agreed, "Yeah, yeah!" One man cried, "Without Jim Jones you wouldn't have life anyway." Rhodes continued,

> Jones was uncannily calm. It was almost impossible to believe that this fanatic was talking coolly and calmly about killing innocent children. . . . It was too insane to comprehend. . . . Jones wanted to hurry things up. He said, "Troops will come in here. They will torture our babies. They will kill everybody. It's better that we die with dignity. . . . I want my babies first."

National Enquirer, December 19, 1978.

. . . And later: "Death is a good thing. It's good to die for something like this. . . . Everything is going to be all right. I am going to be at rest. You will all be at rest, too."*

Clayton and Rhodes reported a combination of voluntary compliance and coercion. The entire event was carried out under the eyes of an armed security force. When the ritual was near completion they lay down their weapons "joining hands with their companions and girlfriends and taking the poison," according to Clayton.

5. The New West Allegations

On August 1, 1977, *New West*, a California magazine, published an article by Marshall Kilduff and Phil Tracy called "Inside People's Temple," addressing the fact that "Jim Jones is one of the state's most politically potent leaders." But, they asked, "Who is he? And what's going on behind his church's locked doors?" To answer the question, the reporters obtained tape-recorded interviews with ten former members. Among the allegations were the following.

(1) *Punishment.* "The first form of punishment was mental where they would get up and totally disgrace and humiliate the person in front of the whole congregation. . . . Jim would then come and put his arms around the person and say, 'I realize you went through a lot, but it was for the cause. Father loves you and you're a stronger person now. I can trust you more now that you've gone through this and accepted this discipline.'" Thus spoke Elmer Myrtle, now Al Mills.

(2) *Deception, intrusion.* Birdie Marable "noticed Jones' aides taking some children aside and asking, what color house did my friend have, things like that. . . . Then during the services Jim called [one woman] out and told her the answers the children had given, as though no one had told him." Mickie

*Ibid.

40

Touchette said she had written letters to various politicians "throughout the state, throughout the country in praise of something they'd done." She told *New West* that she made up aliases.

(3) *Treatment of elderly.* Birdie Marable spoke of conditions on a bus trip from San Francisco to Los Angeles. "It was terrible. It was overcrowded. There were people sitting on the floor, in the luggage rack, and sometimes people [were] underneath in the compartment where they put the bags. I saw something that really put me wise to everything. I saw how they treated old people."

(4) *Frisking of members.* Laura Cornelious said, "You even were asked to raise up on your toes (to check) your shoes."

(5) *Ambitions.* Grace Stoen said, "Jim would say, 'If we stay here in the valley, we're wasted. We could make it to the big time in San Francisco.'"

(6) *A Jones "group session."* Grace Stoen refers to an occasion in San Francisco when "he was having everybody shout Shit! Shit! Shit! to teach them not to be so hypocritical."

(7) *Money issues.* "We had nothing on the outside to get started in. We had given all our money. We had given all our property. We had given up our jobs." (Mertle) Walter Jones said that state money designated for use in a Temple home for disturbed boys was customarily turned over to the Temple. "The church requested that we turn over what remained of the funds. . . . Approximately $900 to $1000 (per month) was turned over to the church. . . . I remember there were times when all the checks were signed over to the church." Laura Cornelious spoke of constant requests for money. "After I was in some time it was made known to us that we were supposed to pay 25 percent of our earnings. . . . He [Jones] said we didn't need the watches—my best watch—he said we didn't need homes—give the homes, furs, all the best things you own."

6. The Rev. Mr. Ross Case

Case, who had known Jones in Indianapolis and also in California, was quoted by Kilduff. "He [Jones] was throwing the Bible on the floor and stepping on the book during services. He was talking on and on about sex. People who wanted to quit his church were worried about getting calls pressuring them to return. We kind of fell out over this."*

7. Wanda Johnson

Wanda Johnson, a former member, described a suicide drill held in San Francisco.

> We were all given wine and if we didn't like it Jones said drink it anyway. They collected the cups and informed us we had just drunk poison and would be dead within 30 minutes. Some people psychologically thought they were dying and fell off their chairs. I felt worried about my baby in Guyana. Jones assured us that they had all been taken care of—killed—and we were all who were left. Across from me, Andy Silvers, one of the few members of the planning commission who knew, jumped up and said, "You mean we're all going to die!" And another member started beating him. Andy fell to the ground and a vial of phony blood spilled to the floor. That's when I knew something wasn't right. One woman ran to die with her baby and she was shot in the side. I thought it was real, but it was a blank. She dropped to the floor. There was a hole in her dress, just to give it reality. . . . [Afterward Jones] told us it was just a test of our loyalty to him. . . . We all knew he was mad, but we were compromised to the point that we could not question him.†

8. Wayne Pietila

Pietila, a former member, said, "When we went down to San Francisco and Los Angeles we were supposed to stand

*Kilduff and Javers, op. cit., p. 29.
†Krause, op. cit., pp. 60-61.

in different parts of the room, posing as bodyguards and occasionally letting our guns show. . . . We used to practice with our weapons."*

9. Assessment of Various Allegations

While several important allegations have been attributed only to a single person, there are also corroborated allegations. The evidence of journalistic reporting and affidavit seems to justify a picture of Jones as a man who went to preposterous lengths to manipulate those around him and to orchestrate impressions of the Temple to the outside world. The most damning and fully corroborated allegation seems to me to be the charge that there were suicide drills well before the end.

From an examination of presently available data, there appears to be a distinct tie between Jones and the culture of popular encounter psychology that erupted during the late sixties, especially in California. I must confess that my own brief brush with sensitivity training was so fraught with malevolent happenings that I rather foolishly told one of the leaders of a weekend I attended that I would not write an explicit account of it. I know myself to be a person resistant to incursions on personal freedom and mobility; yet during that weekend there were aspects of psychic abuse and physical assault that would find a perfectly consistent place in a bill of particulars drawn up against the People's Temple.

How many persons—without substantially questioning the procedure—have willingly submitted themselves to group leaders and processes that were manipulative, coercive, perhaps brutal, not to speak of their being rude—but where the "end" of "happiness" and "liberation" justified the means? Does an alienated America,

*Kilduff and Javers, op. cit., p. 59.

43

particularly its most rootless and alienated territory—California—continue to submit to a whole barrage of psychic incursions on selfhood, generally conducted by amateurs or professionals who have switched from previous employment into group work? The vignette of James Jones sitting with a group in some recess of People's Temple leading a loud chorus of "Shit! Shit!" as a cathartic liberation from "hypocrisy" is all too chillingly similar to much that passes for "therapy" in the so-called sensitivity world.

10. Solidarity Forever

What is impressive, from existing evidence, is the fact that until the end the People's Temple held together, providing a society—increasingly coerced but in some respects content—for a portion of America's dispossessed underclass and alienated privileged. A sense of having been compromised must surely be one explanation why many did not rebel. That and fear of reprisals.

Some doubtless shared a sense of power with their leader. Positive work continued to the end. A few days after the mass deaths, a banquet would have been held in San Francisco to raise money for the Guyana project that boasted a fine record of working with youths who would otherwise have been in jail.

Anyone familiar with family life knows of sudden alterations in moods and appearances. A husband and wife are fighting. Company comes. All is suddenly well. To an extent Jones was able to create the ultimate patriarchal family. It was run on the threat of violence by encouraging the sense that he, Jones, was the benevolent giver of good things. There was a strict discipline. Things got done; people kept in line. This kind of lifestyle is admired by many who lament a bygone day of discipline and order.

The evidence suggests that Jones continually sought to

44

escape scrutiny. As time went on, he began running scared.

Everything he touched seems to have had two sides, a positive surface and a seamy underside. Care for the elderly was tempered with crowding and some lack of concern, even bilking (taking social security payments). There was healing, and also charlatanism. There was tenderness, and brutality. There was public conscientiousness, and private callousness. There was talk of democracy, and rigid control. There was freedom of speech, and crowd coercion.

There is evidence to suggest a caste system within the Temple. There was the largely helpless contingent of elderly blacks. There were middle-class people who gave their energies to the day-to-day maintenance of the church and commune. And there were inner circles around Jones, comprised of the most dangerous element. These would have been avid, intelligent disciples; a militant guard of Marxist idealogues; counselors; strategists; and among them, to be sure, a potentially lethal faction. It may have been this group that helped bring about the final resolution at Jonestown.

11. Survivors

Available evidence does not explain the role of various persons who survived the mass killings. The evidence does not explain the testimony of Terri Buford, a former member, that Tim Stoen, also understood to be a former member, is in fact still an agent of Jones and a dangerous man. Was Buford's testimony part of a post-suicide effort of Jones to destroy Stoen, who had had the gall to take legal action to reclaim a "son" Jones insisted was his? The evidence throws little light on the intricacies of Jones's relations with the U.S. Embassy in Guyana or with the Guyana government proper. Nor do we know whether

Jones was correct in claiming that there were provacateurs within the Temple. It is quite likely that an organization that was militantly espousing the cause of Angela Davis and Huey Newton in the early 1970s may have been the target of investigation at a time when the government was infiltrating virtually any group that seemed radical. It is not at all clear to what extent Jones's paranoia had at least some basis in fact.

Nor do we know who shot Jim Jones.

Finally, there is a large body of evidence yet to be considered. It is the testimony of members themselves that appears in the various "letters to dad," which were published after Jonestown. These letters suggest a psychological dynamic of manipulation in the name of social radicalism. "Dad" was the embodiment of the social ideal of the community, and from this he derived his authority. "Dad" gave them the best life they'd ever known. There must have been quite a bit of probing in public concerning the personal attitudes of members on issues such as "elitism" and "sexual games." There is not a shred of evidence in the letters that there was anything like a religious discipline activating the Guyana communards. It is all devotion to dad and the socialist cause.

12. The End

Finally, though, stands the incomprehensible deed as ultimate evidence. How is it possible that individuals could have accepted the lethal ending? Jones said that "soldiers would come and torture the children." Notice how it is twisted around, blamed on an enemy.

In the end, perhaps, James Jones was partly or wholly stripped of the authority he had held so shakily. He had to rely on sheer power and substantial deception to carry out the final exercise. On the basis of the tape recording that purports to be the actual record of the final event (see

Appendix 21) I must assume that Odell Rhodes's nauseating description is authentic. If so, those who died voluntarily were forced to acquiesce in a ritual of ultimate compromise, a ritual so evil at its base that not even the stern Jehovah of Abraham's time would allow it to come to pass: the sacrifice of the little ones, babies and children. I believed there could hardly be reason to live once one had assented to this, whether by shouts of "Yeah! Yeah!" or by silence. It seemed a grim pact with satanic will and reason. The cries drown out the "revolution" in the suicide. Nihilism triumphs.

There is a suggestion in the *National Enquirer*—a newspaper not generally revered for its accuracy—that a petition was sent to Jones from mothers in Guyana pleading for the lives of their children. If this is true, there were some communards who were aware of the drift of things. Finally, there were a few "no's!" here and there. The tape bespeaks initial resistance. We will never know its extent. Such frail acts of resistance strike one as mere sticks thrown in the face of a whirlwind, and yet they were the only life left at the end.

13. Brainwashing

There is an area of evidence that lies within the purview of social science and psychology. This is mind-control or brainwashing. It has its roots in the treatment of prisoners of war in our century, the training of kamikaze pilots, in the allegations surrounding practices of modern cults. But I think we will accomplish little in the way of understanding Jonestown through use of the idea of brainwashing to account for what happened there. Certainly there were aspects of brainwashing. If some testimony is to be believed, sleep loss occurred, protein was lacking from the diet, and both drugs and corporal punishment were used to prevent defection and "negative behavior." Nevertheless, the term brainwashing obscures rather than illuminates in this instance. The point is that individuals willingly decided to give their lives to the People's Temple. This decision involved a giving up of autonomy and freedom *at the outset* that no amount of brainwashing itself could have achieved. Jones offered a basic alternative to independent living; he gave to people lacking a sense of inner authority a feeling that they were "strong," maybe even "heroic." He put them through "tests"; he wanted to make them "better people," worthy of "the cause." He offered them *meaning* so basic that few voices were raised in defense of an eroding freedom. So, gradually, they were compromised. It was a process other than brainwashing *per se*; something less definable, perhaps, and more horrible. It was not so much a basic strategy for winning new believers as a product of Jones's compulsive need to control his followers. Brainwashing is the effort of one adversary to break down an opposite number. Jones was not the Chinese interrogator trying to break a Yankee officer. He was the shepherd of a willing and often happy flock.

14. Kamikaze Motifs

There is more evidence of a comparative nature to suggest that Jonestown was a semiconscious preparation for mass suicide. If one believes that the formal precipitating cause was the arrival of Congressman Ryan and party, then the determination of Jones, or of his lieutenants, to obliterate them in a way that would seem accidental can only lead to one conclusion: that the rest fell like dominoes. Everything was ready for the last act. The possibility of mass suicide had existed for a year. Perhaps it began to exist when it was no longer possible to conceal the gulf between aggressive behavior and the expectations of Herculean conscience.

> We were forbidden to speak to the women who worked in the kitchen. All correspondence would be censored. [We] did not

have time to read the newspapers or listen to the radio which was in any case forbidden. . . . Like animals who see men for the first time, we gazed curiously at the [visitors]. . . . It was thirty days since we had come in. . . . The enemy was incontestably superior. . . . I . . . was soon to die. [Mother] was condemned to live on with her memories, whereas I, reduced to nothing, would feel neither pain nor joy, and . . . would have no memories. In a sense I was the luckier of the two.

This is not a memoir from Jonestown. It is a seriatim quotation taken from a book called *I Was a Kamikaze* by Ruujii Nagatsuka. "The enemy was incontestably superior. . . . On July 6, both General Saito and Admiral Najami committed suicide. The most frightful scene followed. Soldiers blew themselves up with grenades. Even civilians rushed headlong to their deaths. Some women took their children into their arms and leapt from the cliff tops. . . . Others arm in arm waded out to sea and drowned, rather than submit."

The kamikaze were trained to fight the enemy. Suicide was a by-product of heroic aggression. Striking in Nagatsuka's testimony is the regimentation and isolation of kamikaze training and the link between suicide and the sense of being surrounded by a superior enemy.

According to Deborah Blakey, there was a message delivered to the Guyana government in September 1977, threatening mass suicide if there were an attempt made to give John Victor Stoen into the custody of his parents. Calling frantically from San Francisco, Jones was apparently confident he would command the loyalty of his Guyana commune to the point that it could be used as a weapon in the custody suit, a battle still obscure in origin and a riddle in many respects. *Save that the boy died at Jonestown.* Charles Garry, the San Francisco attorney who escaped the Jonestown carnage, along with Mark Lane, lawyer and conspiracy theorist, said that if it had not been for "that boy," the whole thing would not have happened.

Jones may have gained control over his followers to the point of life and death. But he could not control the outside world's investigating serious charges. Nine hundred souls could be hostaged in Guyana, but the hints were coming. Suicide drills began. The flock became kamikazes, not for the glory of the Empire, surrounded by a real-life enemy; but for the glory of Jim Jones, a martyr to his time, surrounded by fantasy and threat and illness and demonic powers.

It is worth noting that there were days when the original kamikaze planes would take off and find no target and, lacking the wherewithal to return to base, would simply fall into the sea, devoid of glorious encounter with the enemy, an utter waste. There is such an aspect about Jim Jones at the end; a matter-of-factness that has more of compulsive drive than of vision, a will to be done with the whole thing, a possibly American compulsion to make a clean sweep of a bungled job, a need to start over. It is a striking aspect of the Jonestown suicide tape, if it is to be believed: this drivenness reminiscent of a Macbeth turned out on the bleak American prairie.

CHAPTER THREE

James Warren Jones

JIM JONES WON people over with a combination of charm, forcefulness, administrative zeal, and dedication to the cause of a better world. There was a more than substantial constituency for this kind of approach during the 1960s. Kilduff and Javers offer preliminary insights on the sort of authority Jones represented:

> [His] all-embracing philosophy of plenty was particularly enticing to the poor and lower middle class. A promised land where the Temple provided all made them forget about paying the rent and rising food costs. It was a dream to attract those who wanted to forget the realities, leave their tedious jobs and work for the church.
> For others, it was relief from desperate problems of ill-health. An older woman or man who could barely understand the medical jargon of a busy doctor was comforted by the patient, solicitous Jones. The Sunday morning excitement of a People's Temple service was much like the gospel-singing churches in the South and Midwest, where many of the older members had grown up.
> Daily Temple life was simple. Church members were stripped of their money, private life and outside friends—not to speak of the terrifying complexities of the world. They had only to follow Jones's commands. . . .
> Finally, there was his personality. Jones was a master manipulator. . . . [His] changeable nature, at one moment full

51

of promise, in the next depraved and self-pitying, was simply overpowering.*

That description is very much like the mythic Hercules.

He considered himself on an equality with the gods. . . . Throughout his life Hercules had this perfect confidence that no matter who was against him he could never be defeated. . . . Whenever he fought with anyone the issue was certain beforehand. He could be overcome only by a supernatural force. . . . His intellect was not strong. His emotions were. They were quickly aroused and apt to get out of control. . . . He had sudden outbursts of furious anger which were always fatal to the often innocent objects. When the rage would pass and he would come to himself he would show a most disarming penitence and agree humbly to any punishment it was proposed to inflict on him. . . . He spent a large part of his life expiating one unfortunate deed after another and never rebelling against the almost impossible demands made on him. Sometimes he punished himself when others were inclined to exonerate him. By his sorrow for wrongdoing and his willingness to do anything to expiate it, he showed greatness of soul. If only he had had some greatness of mind also, at least enough to lead him along the ways of reason, he would have been the perfect hero.†

In early manhood, Hercules goes mad and slays his wife and children. He seeks to slay himself but is restrained by Theseus. "So be it," Hercules responds. "I will be strong and wait for death." He sets out to expiate his wrongs and undertakes prodigious labors. He completes the necessary course of expiation but does not stop. Along with good deeds there are careless lapses. He kills a boy accidentally; he slays a good friend to avenge a father's insult. He is

*Marshall Kilduff and Ron Javers, *Suicide Cult* (New York, 1978), pp. 68-69.
†Edith Hamilton, *Mythology* (Boston: Little, Brown & Co., 1942), pp. 160ff.

always undergoing some form of penance. Death comes at last. He is "murdered" but will not die. ("He could still slay others," Hamilton recounts, "but it seemed that he himself could not die.") In the end he wills to take his own life. A pyre is prepared, and Hercules dies in the enveloping flames.

In James Jones, Herculean conscience is wed to a character riddled with ambivalence: he is a hardworking minister but exults in what a racket religion can be; he rails about sexual morality but boasts to his attorney of the number of liaisons he has had, with men and women, in a single day; he proclaims himself in favor of civil rights but dwells morbidly on the scenario of racial holocaust in the presence of his largely black congregation. Eventually he paints a picture of American death camps to lure them to Guyana.

Jones most often gets his way, even at the price of painful self-mortification. It is the infantile mechanism of over-weening self-will, which always carries with it the implicit threat of self-destruction. It begins in seemingly harmless acts of self-pity and self-indulgence.

How much of what happened at Jonestown was the product not so much of malevolent design but of a logical, almost inevitable, characterological evolution of self-pity? Self-pity is a common strategem in America, particularly among men, and its mirror image is a sometimes bluff, sometimes blatant, "hail-fellow-well-met" aggression. There is occasionally to be found, in addition, a sort of instant apocalyptic attitude of hopelessness. At the end Jones seems a far cry from the Marxist revolutionary advocating mass suicide as a contribution to the socialist cause. He is more like Bob Dylan's evocation of a man named Hollis Brown. Hollis Brown is the archetype of the victimized father of many children. In ultimate despair, he resolves matters not by lashing out but by turning his anger inward. Finally he kills his wife, his children, and himself.

Dylan's Hollis Brown lives on the outside of town. All the forces of society are ranged against him. He has prayed, but there was no answer. He looked for a friend, but there was no one. He spends his last money on seven shotgun shells. His preoccupation with death grows daily. It begins to burn inside him. Finally he can bear it no longer. He takes the gun and uses it. Resolution comes: thus the Lacan-described "revenge of massive proportions." Or is it simply a twisted assumption of humiliated patriarchy?*

We do not know and perhaps will never know whether James Jones was criminally insane at the time he ordered the deaths and suicides. He sounds both logical *and* mad on the death tape.

The following represents a portion of what we know of James Warren Jones.

Born: May 13, 1931.

Father: James Jones, gassed in World War I, cannot work. Age forty-seven at James's birth. He dies when James is an adolescent.

Mother: Lynetta, primary support of family, works in factory at odd jobs; age thirty at James's birth. She indulges him.

Home: Lynn, Indiana. Pop. 1350. Chief industry: caskets

Status: Poor.

Environment: Racist, Bible Belt.

Early religious affiliation: Nazarene.

Character as a child: Loner. Living in the shadow of a powerless, sometimes hostile, Klan-oriented father and a mother with reputation for strength, defiance of social

---

*A study could be made on the hypothesis that dictatorial persons seem to reach a "point" at which early, suppressed impulses are acted out. The "point" corresponds to the moment that enough power is acquired to satisfy a basic ambition. Thereafter the tendency seems to be not only toward destruction but severe misjudgments, which help surround the dictator with hostile forces requiring a suicidal response.

custom, resiliency. Growing determination to be a leader. Strong temper; has mother's proficiency at cursing. Concern for downtrodden.

Education, development: Little known. Remains quiet, aloof. Religious interests predominate; must work to make ends meet. Average intelligence by IQ standards.

Marriage: In 1949, marries Marceline Baldwin, a nurse, two to four years his senior. Marceline is given to impulsive acts of charity. Jones enrolls in Butler University, 1950. Seen by one contemporary as maladjusted, overly dependent on Marceline.

Character as young man (confused by conflicting evidence): In a *New York Times* interview in 1977, Marceline claims that Jones has been Marxist since the time of their marriage and that Mao is his hero. During the 1950s he serves as an occasional preacher, then full minister, in a series of churches in Indianapolis. Is effective and darkly handsome. Relates biblical faith to social issues, particularly racism. Leaves Methodist Church because he finds it too "racist." Forms his own racially inclusive congregation in 1953.

Development of career: People's Temple affiliates as one of the autonomous member congregations of the Disciples of Christ in 1960. Jones is ordained as a Disciples of Christ minister in 1964. Allegation of false healings extend to this period; also stories of legitimate ones. Assistance to poor continues; during the 1960s, Jones becomes a political force in Indianapolis, serving as the city's first Human Relations Commissioner. Visits Father Divine, returns a changed man. Wishes to be called father.

Personal: First and only child born to Marceline and James: Stephan Gandhi Jones, in 1961. During the early 1960s the couple begins adopting children to form an interracial family group. There are also allegations of Jones's sexual disaffection with Marceline at this time and commencement of his liaisons with younger women in his congregation.

More career: Jones begins a pattern to last the rest of his life: when threatened, he leaves. In face of one church member's threat to investigate claims of faith healings, Jones plans to depart for California with a portion of his flock. Jones manifests an increasingly autocratic style softened by a power of "sincere concern" that overwhelms. Establishes an interrogation committee to deal with critics. There are investigations of personal real estate transactions involving church-owned property.

Jones has by now developed into a highly effective orator who frequently adopts a Billy Graham "The *Bible* says . . ." stance in the pulpit. In 1965 he prophesies nuclear disaster—dating it July 17, 1967—and leads some seventy followers to Redwood Valley in Mendocino County, California, to avoid the predicted doom. The congregation is fully integrated, about half black. The *New York Times* biography (November 26, 1978) refers to Jones's "intelligence, soft-spoken friendliness and seemingly earnest search for a better world" at this time. A local California judge, Robert Winslow, recalled, "He was a very bright, humanistic person. He didn't seem to be a socialist. They were nice, concerned people. Their most significant characteristic was that they wanted to come to the aid of anyone in trouble. Jones wasn't a fanatic when I knew him, although people were emotionally dependent on him."

The people in his community build their entire lives around Jones and the church.

There was a turning point. Timothy and Grace Stoen became members. Stoen is a well-respected liberal attorney; his joining helps legitimize the church in the community. Following the assassination of Martin Luther King, Jr., Stoen sells most of his possessions and turns the proceeds over to Jones. There is a continuing, still obscure, tie between Jones, Timothy, and Grace.

In 1971 Jim Jones moves operations to San Francisco. He works hard; he organizes his thirteen-bus fleet in a single day to form a caravan. Politicians, liberal and radical, look to him as an ally. But as the People's Temple grows and appears to flourish, the inner picture seems to change. Some say Jones has become a monster. There are boasts of sexual prowess, sexual liaisons with men and women in the church, explicit rejections of the Bible, admiring statements about Hitler and Lenin. A visible armed cadre of protectors develops, Jones speaks of a coming race war, with blacks suffering a fate analogous to the Jews in World War II. Members complain about their fatigue following various tasks set by Jones. There are smaller and larger acts of sadism. An aberrant member is paddled in public. Then there is Jones's arrest in Hollywood in 1973 on a lewd conduct charge. These negative happenings accompany his public emergence as a shining moral example. Lester Kinsolving, an Episcopal journalist-priest, writes a series of highly critical articles about Jones and People's Temple. In early 1973, Kinsolving produces a column criticizing the Disciples of Christ natonal leadership for refusing to investigate Jones. There is a flurry of concern, but the denomination does not act; People's Temple launches counter-publicity campaign. (See Appendix.) Shortly after Jones's arrest and the Kinsolving uproar, a group from People's Temple goes to Guyana to scout out possibilities of a major move.

Jones appear to be a vociferous champion of the free press, supporting with demonstrations and dollars the journalistic community. He has direct control of some two thousand people in the San Francisco area and, according to Tim Stoen, can deliver them to a polling place or anywhere else in the city within six hours. Jones demands, as did Father Divine before him, the complete allegiance of followers, including the turning over of assets. Up to 40 percent of the gross income of parishioners is claimed. Many sell their homes and donate the proceeds.

Around Jones there is an omnipresent guard, an omnipresent entourage. He is on the left, courting the likes of George Moscone, who wins the mayoral election and appoints Jones to the housing commission. But as public notice increases, the facade begins to crumble. Negative images surface among discontented followers: Jones is a "fraud," a "manipulator," a man whose poses and secrecies are so much a part of him that it is impossible to gauge the real, at least until the roof caves in over the fissure. In 1977, under growing media pressure, Jones takes his remaining followers to Guyana.

Even the relatively simple exercise of excerpting from available data some salient features of Jones's life thrusts one deeper and deeper into tortured mazes of unreality, self-indulgence, and messianic dreams. Somehow, to take that integrated "model" community with him, to preserve it as an emblem of a better world, becomes for Jones a pearl of great price. Jones is an effective orator who can thump the Bible and ring out an impressive list of cries in the wilderness: Amos, Jeremiah, John the Baptist, Sojourner Truth, W. E. B. DuBois, Engels, Lenin, Marx. He does so in a disarming voice that has the accents of the Midwest, of California radicalism, of black preaching. Most of all, on the tape, he sounds like Harry Truman—the nuances are farm-belt American. Jones has power to make people give him everything. His are not the consolations of an Aimee Semple McPherson, Billy Sunday, Billy Graham, or Leighton Ford—none of whom really ever pretended to be anything other than what they were. One clue to the difference between Jones and these others lies in the banality of the rewards he allows himself, a dismal dirge of tiny privileges won: an extra roll of toilet paper, extra meat, a deception over the number of shoes he actually owns, bulletproof bus compartment, shabby sexual prerogatives. Like a trusty in a prison of his own making, Jones wrings small concessions because ultimately he is the slave of his ambivalent conscience.

It is Jones's fate to live in an apocalyptic age. It becomes increasingly hard for him to maintain a rational, balanced prophetic faith amid assassinations, the endless cold war, nuclear development, and the flaky world of California radicalism. He rationalizes his human lapses—his probable alienation from his spouse; his attraction to younger women; his lust, here and there, for a male. This is the James Jones of a middle-aged stomach and a full medicine chest. He is hypochondriacal and drug-dependent, stamping on the Bible and claiming that he, Jim Jones, would make a better God than the One who inhabits the pages of that book.

Confusion, parody, charades, a veritable culture clash of irreconcilable styles and devices: Yet Jim Jones somehow holds them all together. He is in this respect a tragic hero of sorts.

How strong in Jim Jones were the images of Marx, Lenin, and Stalin? Did he have a real commitment to the world socialist revolution? Or was it just a fashionable latching on to the rhetoric of opposition to the American system? Did he struggle to survive as a Communist in capitalist America? If Marceline Jones is to be believed, Jones was a Marxist from the beginning. A memo allegedly in his own hand speaks of the early 1950s, saying that, at the time, Jones was wondering whether Stalin was as bad as Americans said he was. Jones was evidently angry, too, at any form of anti-Semitism, incensed to the point of suicidal identification with the execution of the Rosenbergs.

Suppose for a moment that he was a true Communist. What does that do to our entire perception of Jim Jones? Everything he did could then be fit into the dialectic of the cold war. Visceral anti-Communism is, after all, standard, even today, in the United States.

If Jones was a committed Communist, certain things fall into place. It helps explain why Jones was publicly opposed to racial segregation well before 1954 and the Brown vs. Board of Education decision striking down the "separate but equal" clause. It is doubtful that Jones learned his integrationist credo from the white churches he attended and preached in as a young man. It is quite possible that he acquired an affinity with the American Communism of the period, whose position was consistently opposed to racism. It is also possible he picked up some socialist views as a lower-class child growing up in the Midwest. In the 1930s, socialism and pacifism were in the air far more than in the 1940s and 1950s.

Marxism undoubtedly played a fundamental role in Jones's thinking, along with other influences and drives: Christianity, black messianism, overweening personal ambition, fringe religious notions, and not least a growing sense of his own power to manipulate people for his own ends. It is also probable that Jones drew committed Marxist-oriented radicals into his California circle in the 1960s and 1970s. There seems little doubt that, at the end, the People's Temple of the Disciples of Christ was at the same time a professed effort to exemplify collective living along the model of agrarian socialism—and that Jones had largely rejected Christianity for Communism.

It should be noted that Marxism promulgated and echoed many of the prophetic elements of biblical faith, fusing these into a revolutionary program whose goal is the achievement of the kingdom of God on earth by violent means. What makes Marx attractive to present-day intellectuals, in the West particularly, is that he did envision a world beyond alienation, materialism, and class oppression.

In one of the most significant movements of our time, Marxism and Christianity became implacable enemies, to the vast detriment of both. Marxism helped to topple autocratic power and replace it with new, often horribly repressive, regimes committed to state socialism. Christianity at the same time became gutted of its social message and was relegated to the role of nonauthoritative chaplain of the capitalist classes, largely ignoring the reigning politics.

By now this opposition has largely run its course. There is a search for a compromise between the Marxism of "bloody revolution" and a Christianity of jingoistic support of "freedom," which in some cases means little more than an affirmation of the status quo.

It is essential for the survival of religious institutions that the prophetic torch torn from their bosom by Marxism be reclaimed. This violent rupture left biblical faith trivialized and eviscerated. Only in this way can religious institutions play a culturally transforming role in the world's future.

A century ago Eleanor Marx, Karl Marx's youngest daughter, told an audience of Chicago workers that to her socialism meant

> giving property to the thousands and millions who today have none, . . . law that is justice, and is just to all men and women . . . to give all men and women a chance of developing, of bringing out what is best in them. . . . We want to do away with the proletariat class, . . . we want to do away with all class distinctions, and while we say, all men and women shall perform their share of the necessary labor of the world, we also say that they shall enjoy a fair share of leisure and pleasure. . . . We are told that "socialists want to have women in common." Such an idea is possible only in a society that looks upon women as a commodity."*

In the near century since those words were uttered, we have witnessed the rise of the Soviet and American superpowers. Concurrently, ecological reality is pushing us to a spaceship earth concept that renders obsolete the struggle between these two powers. Both powers would—

*Yvonne Kupp, *Eleanor Marx*, Vol. 2 (New York, 1976), pp. 162-64.

or should—subscribe to the fundamentally Christian social ideals enunciated by Eleanor Marx.

The task of religious institutions is to seize and preserve a core of transcendental values. Crying peace—peace where there is no peace—is no answer in these times. Working to ensure human rights and to articulate human obligations of tolerance, enablement, and democracy is a platform to occupy religious institutions now and in days to come.

Jim Jones was an emotional Marxist. Marxism was, for him, a means of polarizing the world into Good and Bad. The possibilities of a Communist revolution in the United States are no greater now than they were a hundred years ago.

What seems certain today is the continued growth of a mixed economy throughout the Communist and capitalist worlds. Equally certain is the growth of the Third World, far removed from the material blessings of life that have fallen to the heirs of Karl Marx and Adam Smith. The task is not to divide but to unite to meet new challenges to justice and human survival.

The issue of Jones's Marxism is confusing. The Guyana commune could be viewed as a socialist experiment, a primitive effort at Skinnerian mind-control, a testing ground exploring the effects of thorazine and other powerful drugs among a wide population, a totalitarian regime, a paternalistic family camp, or even as a base for the aggrandizement of substantial power in a developing country. The degree of Jones's inner madness, the question of his basic thought processes, the possibility that the man carried within him a veritable jukebox machine full of appropriate rhetoric—all these militate against a clear portrait of his Marxism.

Up to the end, Jones clearly remained a powerful man. Power is never one-sided; it is always reciprocal. It requires an object, a compliant entity. Jones was able to gather People's Temple to himself in a penumbra of love. It was his vast extended family. He was emboldened to take the name of father. But even here he forswore a certain traditional dignity. The name contracted to dad.

It is very telling that the form of People's Temple was "family." We are, above all, a society of *institutions:* churches, schools, prisons, nursing homes, mental hospitals. Even the arts and entertainment have an institutional pallor: civic centers, "grants," universities. The irony is that now the state and bureaucratic mechanisms—concerned about alienation from these institutions—are taking a renewed interest in the only face-to-face social entity left: the family. The family must be strengthened, say the experts. Marriages need to be repaired. Children need parents who can provide them with care not obtainable even in the best institutions. From the *National Review* to the writings of Christopher Lasch, the chorus is similar: narcissistic America, bombed out in the 1960s, ego-bathed in the 1970s, must recover itself. Implication: restore the patriarchal family. The weak father provides a climate of alienation, today's father is a "grass bent by the winds." Forward to a nonfeminist, patriarchal restoration!

Jim Jones was a down-the-line patriarch. "Do as dad says. Dad knows best" was the chorus of his followers. He attracted fragmented souls who needed the regulation of a patriarchal order. The power of the crowd, of Jones's oratory, washed over their bruised parts. They were drawn—like solitary cells—into an organism. Those that betrayed a hint of resistance or doubt formed a curious threat to Jim Jones, rather like cancer. (Jones's cancer fears heightened whenever there was danger of exposure, and by the end he was dying of cancer in his mind.) But Jim Jones broke down the recalcitrant cells, slicing through their cortical layers, engrafting human being after human being. After a certain point his actions became silly, disgusting, repulsive, compromising, a travesty. He became a sort of Banana Republic spiritual dictator with caravans of sleepless acolytes shuttling the freeways of California. Herculean conscience provided the necessary prod. If not a vote for George Moscone, a socialist utopia in Guyana! If not a socialist utopia, a "revolutionary" death. All in the name of patriarchal love!

When investigators dared to say that Jones had done wrong, the wounded entity departed for the rain forests of northern Guyana. Jones was by now sick unto death. It followed that the others must be sick also. At night he harangued his followers, vacillating between a tawdry self-pity and a steadfastness of devotion to Marx, Lenin, and agrarian socialism. But it is in the nature of power, beyond a certain point, to make mistakes. It is a reaction to real or imagined enemies. Full speed ahead to Moscow! became the cry. But Moscow would not have the Temple. Down with the foreign relations committee! But the defectors kept the pressure on, and Congressman Ryan went to Guyana. Doom drew nearer with every breath.

The first Guyana defections coincided with the ending in America of the miasmal sleep of the 1970s. There was a glimmer in the United States of an awakening from the cult netherworld, presidential deposings, painful memories. There was disaffection from embarrassingly shallow retreats into pop psychology. But Jones had lost contact. Isolation bred only isolation. And so the defectors came to provide Jones with a *raison d'etre,* an edge, even a plan of action. The wheels of investigation were in motion. The drama's last act was begun. The Stoens wanted their "son" John-John. Hatreds were present amid the "love." Let me alone, cried Jim Jones. John-John is mine! But they are coming! The end is near! The self-swallowing father, the law-unto-self, is finally left alone with his family of misfits, colluded cells, and alienated brothers and sisters. He is left at last with a mass of drugged, trapped, and sleepless cells who call him dad. It's his own body. Here, at the ends of the earth, there is hardly a question of doing it differently.

64

CHAPTER FOUR

Jesus

THERE WAS SO much reference to James Jones as a "messiah figure" following Jonestown that it is almost inevitable that people would question any form of messianism; even that of one whose attitudes Jones came to reject with increasing vigor, Jesus of Nazareth. If there is any providence in Jonestown, it may be to impress upon us the way in which Jesus contrasts not only with Jim Jones but with all self-appointed messiahs. For Jesus is emphatically *not* the Messiah, either in the sense understood by his enemies or in the modern sense of the messianic religious or political leader.

Jesus was not the promised deliverer of the Jews. He was not a temporal spiritual-military charismatic who gathered the people into an army to throw off the yoke of foreign domination. He was not a Garibaldi, George Washington, or St. Joan.

The first word to describe Jesus is teacher: one who has wisdom to impart. Both his disciples and his enemies call him "Rabbi." It is the most common description of Jesus and in many ways the most accurate.

Jesus is also a prophet. He sees himself as such, as do both his followers and his opponents.

He is also the "Son of man." This is rather a special term, affirming common humanity. It also refers to one who will come in the future, to the perfected humanity that Jesus embodies.

Above all, Jesus comes as a servant. He exposes messianic illusions. He rejects the glib promises of the kingdoms of power. The suffering servant of Isaiah 53, who is ultimately rejected and despised, wounded for our transgressions, is the prefiguring of Jesus.

Jesus is proclaimed at every point *in relationship to God*, not as an alternative to God. When people try to turn him into an object of worship, he affirms a basic monotheism: only God is to be worshiped. When Satan refers to Jesus as God's Son, Jesus puts the designation into proper context by affirming the first commandment: You shall worship God alone.

Jesus sees himself as a prophet. He is heir to the Old Testament prophet-poets. He comes to proclaim liberty to the oppressed, release to captives, sight to the blind, the acceptable year of the Lord.

Jesus is also a leader. But the shape and scope of his leadership divide it radically from the idea of messiahship, at least as that idea was (and is) generally held. The essense of Jesus' leadership lies in his teachings; the focus is not allegiance to himself but the proclamation of a developing realm of redemption.

Healing and casting out demons are signs of this unfolding new era. Jesus' teaching is by precept and example and parable. He does not build an institution with himself as the center. For Jesus, the proper worship of God is not to cry, "Lord, Lord!" but always "to do the will of my Father which is in heaven."

One key to an understanding of Jesus lies in Peter's so-called "confession" in the Synoptic Gospels (Matt. 16, Mark 8, and Luke 9).*

Jesus asks his disciples who the people say the Son of man is. They reply that some see him as a reincarnation of

---

*I am indebted to Walter Wink for a helpful clarification of this passage, though I should add he is not responsible for my interpretation.

John the Baptist, others as Elijah, others as one of the Old Testament prophets. He then asks the same question directly of his disciples. Peter says in all three versions, "You are the Christ." Which is to say, the Messiah. In Matthew this is followed by the text that forms the biblical basis for the Roman papacy. Jesus will build his church upon "this rock," i.e., Peter.

Mark and Luke pass immediately to an emphatic response by Jesus: He charged them to tell this to no one [Luke]. He charged them to tell no one about him [Mark]. Then he strictly charged the disciples to tell no one he is the Christ [Matthew]. This can hardly be taken as a summons to tactful silence. Quite the contrary, it can be seen as a realization on Jesus' part that the disciples have done the one thing that utterly destines his mission to earthly failure. Jesus has been totally, even fatally, misunderstood.

Why else would Jesus now, for the first time, teach the disciples that he must go to Jerusalem, suffer many things, be rejected by the political and religious establishment, be killed, and on the third day rise again? This is his true destiny, the very story upon which ultimate faith is to be based. It is the gospel story. It is the foundation of what is truly good news; that finally the reality of evil, sin, and death is conquered! It totally rejects the messianic image.

What, we might ask, is Peter's reaction? What of this rock-like figure who must undergo many wracking transformations before he finally understands the true scope of Jesus' life and ministry? What does he say? According to Matthew and Mark, Peter, the proud erroneous confessor, has a sort of seizure. He has just cheered a crucial Superbowl touchdown in the last seconds of play only to see, at his elation's height, the umpire raise a flag to proclaim that the battle appears lost, the gamble hopeless. Peter grabs Jesus, crying out (in Matthew), "God forbid, Lord! This shall never happen to you!" And Jesus immediately rebukes him, "You are not on the side of God, but of men. Get thee behind me, Satan!" *Jesus is incarnate authority saying no! to power*. How clear can it be? How close to his original rejection of Satan's alluring temptation! Thou shalt worship God alone; God only shall you serve!

Coclimactic with the event just described is the transfiguration. This event conveys an indisputable reality: that Jesus, far from fulfilling the role of the Messiah armed with power and the sword, is in fact the true holy one of God, one to whom all humanity must listen. And I stress *listen*. In the Synoptic Gospels, the crucial sentences recur at the moment of transfiguration: "Listen to him." "Hear him." His words transform the old law. "Behold, I make all things new."

After the transfiguration, Jesus begins to refer to himself as a "Servant." He comes closer and closer to the vision of Isaiah 53. He is the very antithesis of the messianic leader. Everything works in just the opposite way. He is gradually stripped of the modest power he has, convicted in the most humiliating way possible, condemned to die a criminal's death. Most of his disciples are not even present at Golgotha. He is truly the forsaken one. Yet by his stripes, says Isaiah, we are healed.

Jesus is the bearer of God's will for us, not the Messiah who will bring about the realm of redemption by power. Thus we must be wary of the church's repeating Peter's initial error of greeting Jesus uncritically as Messiah and of perpetuating the very blindness that Jesus came to heal. The coming of the Holy Spirit, which reinstates the possibility of a universal language, confirms that human beings are to operate by the very faith that Jesus advocates. They are to embody the vision of a world made whole, of a life made abundant. The coming of the Holy Spirit implies the democratization of the messianic vision and its universal spread. *What is not implied is the organization of a church that appropriates various norms of biblical messianism and applies them to the person of the risen Christ*. Jesus as the Christ or Messiah can represent only the one whom we believe to be the incarnation of a God who wills to defeat the messianic mentality by bestowing a faith by which humanity can realize its full destiny and power.

There are, of course, great barriers impeding the proclamation of the gospel. We are just beginning to emerge from a long winter of static biblical scholarship. In 1906, Albert Schweitzer published the book that set the stage for half a century of indifference to Gospel narrative as a living source of inspiration to the church. It was called *The Quest for the Historical Jesus.* Schweitzer argued that it was impossible to come up with a valid, consistent view of Jesus as a historical figure. Citing various works of criticism and textual analysis, he concluded that Jesus' main mission was to propound the imminent end of the world. Across the span of centuries, such a view of Jesus renders him inaccessible as a living, breathing historical figure. Indeed, Schweitzer called Jesus "the unknown."

Schweitzer's own solution was to propound a derivative (and somewhat paternalistic) faith based on "reverence for life." Today the work of perceiving Jesus is served by pointing up the limitations of Schweitzer's approach. A tangible Jesus emerges in the gospel story, disturbing not because he is vague but because he is explicit. The biblical Jesus is hard to listen to. He speaks of radical forgiveness, simple prayer, acts of mercy, and the probability that active faith will meet with official discontent. He is certainly as tangible as the Old Testament prophets, leading to a suspicion that the reason Schweitzer's view has been so well accepted is that it is most convenient for a privileged church to assume that Jesus did not mean what he was clearly saying. George Bernard Shaw was not off the mark when he suggested that the only problem with Christianity was that no one had ever tried it.

To hear the words of Jesus is to be led into a holistic

understanding of the relationship between biblical vision and the world. The only authentication of the *church as an institution* is as bearer of this story. Even the powerful symbols of baptism and Holy Communion summonses to repentance and new life are meaningful only in relation to the story that they recall.

A hint of the holistic vision of the story can be gathered from the following outline. It is but one way of telling it, derived from my own musical efforts:

1. Strange births. Elizabeth and Mary are precursors of a new era. To Mary is given the prophetic song:

> My soul magnifies the Lord
> The fulfilling time has come
> The scattering time has come
> The mercy time has come
> And the time has come when the hungry
> Shall be hungry no more.*

Mary says that the high and mighty will be toppled from their thrones. Jesus is the incarnation not of a political messiah but of one who will make the terms of the prophetic Jeremiah realizable by conquering sin and death and by sending the Holy Spirit.

2. Conventional blood relationships, the patriarchal line, are supplanted by a crucial assertion: Those who hear and do the word of God are related.

3. This coming into the world of Jesus is to fulfill a prophecy that runs counter to conventional notions of *power* as the efficacious agent of salvation. In place of power there is the *authority* of one of whom Isaiah said:

> Who has believed what we have heard?
> To whom is God revealed?

*These and subsequent lyrics are from Stephen Rose, *New Rain: The Story of Jesus in Song* and *A Stranger Named Peace*. © 1977-1978 Persephone Music ASCAP.

He shall raise up a tender plant
Yet we shall not desire it.

Light of the world, of Mary born
Our sorrows yet he'll bear
We see him stricken, afflicted so
Wounded for our transgressions.

Wounded for the wrongs we've done
Like sheep we've turned away
And on his shoulders God has laid
The pain of all our straying.

4. The arrival of Jesus sets in motion the response of power. Herod tries to turn the wise men into secret agents. They refuse. He unleashes revenge—the slaughter of the innocents. Jesus escapes. This defines the tension within the redemptive process—applause at escape, anger at innocent suffering. In history this will create the age of Herculean conscience.

5. Mary becomes a forgotten woman whose story is largely unrecorded. There is an implication that her story waits to be fully told. We must not suppress it.

6. John heralds the coming of the adult Jesus, carrying the prophetic denunciation to a point of nearly unbearable extremity.

You brood of vipers
You lost generation
You cry out to Abraham
You think you are a nation
That can stand when the world is all on fire
But where are those among you
Who wouldn't plunder enemies
Take food from babies
Bow to the emperor
Where are those among you who can stand?

But the one who comes after me
Is a mightier one than I
I'll wash you with water
He'll lead you to the fire
Ah, the love that he brings
Is a love to bind the wounds that you can't heal
The power that he brings is a power
No power on earth can steal

Oh, sometimes I'd like to take my people to the town
Cry out THE END!
See the walls all come a-tumbling down
But we are too few
And there's nothing we can do
But wait for the day when the crooked paths are straight
Let the mountains bow down and the valleys
all rise
Mountains bow down and the valleys all rise and the people in
surprise
Rise up to greet their liberating lord.

7. Jesus comes upon the scene and suffers temptation by Satan. Satan, like the demons, knows that Jesus is the one who has come to sow unity where Satan has bred division. The battle is joined on the spot. Jesus refuses the weapons of power.

8. Healing is the first manifestation of the authority of Jesus, the visible sign of his proclamation of the new age. The touch of his hand brings new life to all who approach him. He calls his followers to share in the healing task.

9. Teaching is the second manifestation of Jesus' authority—he is the messenger of God's law for the new age.

> Blessed are the poor in spirit
> Blessed are those who mourn
> Blessed the tormented
> And those who suffer scorn

Blessed are the merciful
And those whose hearts are pure
Blessed the tormented
And blessed are the poor

10. Confrontation with scribes and Pharisees comes because of Jesus' healing—which is said to usurp God's place—and because of his teaching—which suggests a stringent new code and at the same time mercy and forgiveness mediated not through the priesthood but among people themselves, reciprocally.

11.   He had a dream that God had decided
That the dawn of a new day was near
When the Lord's mighty hand would deliver the land
From legions, false temples, and fear.

He rode to the city, he rode to the temple
At the head of a people's parade
Cried out to the priests for the people's release
And plans for his death they were laid.

12.   So they nailed him to nothingness
Beneath a restless sky
Where is your power
The tollkeeper cried
And laughing at the slave
Who'd assume a master's way
They lay that dead madman in the grave
Thunder of emptiness weeping
At the end of the road.

Down by the graveside the women were weeping
And the tollkeeper's minions they surveyed the pain
But the grave could not contain the body of *that* slave
And the wall of time it was broken again.
He's walking free on the highway
We could travel that way.

There are many ways, of course, to tell the story. And each part of the story is a world in itself. But on fundamental realities is there not agreement among those who read the texts? Agreement about the strangeness of the Advent? The terms of Jesus' arrival? The healing, the teaching, the confrontations? The wrestling with evil and death that came after passing through the state and the juridical system? The resurrection? A fearsome event, hardly intelligible to a world that will not accept miracle, though miracle sustains us. Is all this a dream, a figment of imagination?

Our world is not at odds with the story. The story rather illuminates the world and makes it comprehensible. To the extent that the story itself becomes our focus there is an inherent corrective to the temptation to stray into a fatal dialectic or lapse into the impossibilities of Herculean conscience. Jesus is not Schweitzer's unknown; but our Teacher, Healer, Confronter, Suffering Servant, and risen Troubadour of life. The story is not about an unattainable world but about the ecological necessities of survival and evolution to full humanity.

When Jesus (and the story) is forgotten or suppressed, false Christs rise up. But they cannot supplant him. They witness to him in their failures, in their compromise with evil powers. The day of the Lord is postponed, but not denied.

CHAPTER FIVE

Father Divine

THE PRIVILEGED CLASSES of the United States have a highly developed ability to rationalize experience. This is a difficulty in confronting Jonestown. A largely scientific world view compels the educated to seek logical connections and logical reasons when faced with the irrational. But there is an underclass in America. There is a pool of those who are neither workers nor consumers. We have evolved a welfare system that does not cope with this basic reality, and thus we salve our conscience in the face of human and social waste.

The underclass is always economically depressed. It is a mostly black population. It formed the core of Jones's congregation. Earlier in this century, a man who claimed to be "god in the flesh" appeared to this population. This man was in all probability Jones's model. His name was Father Divine.

Some say his real name was George Baker and that he was born near Savannah, Georgia, around 1875. But as a young man he was drawn to some black preachers who claimed to be God, and he learned from them and improved on them. And by 1915 he had founded his own Peace Mission Movement. He became God. He called for complete submission of his followers. They turned over all they owned. They lived cooperatively. He supplied food and shelter. Racial equality prevailed. So did celibacy. So did strict standards of personal morality.

Divine's first commune, or "heaven," was in Sayville, New York; but the movement grew to some 170 "heavens," mainly in New York and Philadelphia. Perhaps ten thousand joined. Father Divine died in 1965. The movement declined.

James Jones visited Father Divine in Philadelphia in the early 1960s. He came back, by several accounts, a changed man. There were important differences, to be sure. Divine was black; Jones white (though he claimed Indian blood through his mother). Divine openly proclaimed himself God. Jones was more self-effacing, at least in public. Divine remained a staunch defender of the Bill of Rights, the Constitution, and the American legal system; Jones ultimately indicted all American society. Divine proclaimed himself immortal but died; Jones said he was dying and advocated revolutionary suicide. But both men shared a conviction of the injustice of racism. Both were driven by the immediate need to move beyond this unjust state of affairs.

As God, Divine said he was the source of all. Money was no longer necessary to the believer. Turn over all you have to God. And God will provide. So Divine provided free meals; not merely soup kitchen meals but vast, elaborate banquets accompanied by worship of himself, ecstatic worship of a God five feet tall in the midst of his chosen ones. Buses moved back and forth from Sayville to Harlem.

Divine was soon harassed by his staid suburban white neighbors. He was called into court for disturbing the peace. The judge, clearly prejudiced, threw the book at him. It was a costly throw. Soon after the trial, the judge dropped dead; and Father Divine—who had long since learned that unless God is omnipotent, others are likely to usurp his place—claimed immense powers of retribution. "I hated to do it," he said. The judge's death was but a sample of his powers. Divine was released on a successful appeal only a month after sentencing. The next day at a welcome-back banquet his following grew to two thousand. He moved to Harlem.

By the 1930s Divine came into his own. A parsimonious approach to discipleship enabled him to amass wealth which he never owned, being God. The wealth was poured into real estate and small businesses. Purchases, even of large hotels, were always in cash. There were bigger banquets, more free meals, and residences where one could live for almost nothing. His following grew apace. Divinism matured into a theological system.

This modest, bald man was God. His various centers were heavens. He was the source of all, to be obeyed completely. His powers of retribution became, if anything, more formidable with time: It was

the most certain way he was able to evolve for keeping his followers entirely submissive. There are a few followers in the movement who would wish to return to the outside world but who dare not attempt to divorce themselves. . . . They stay in heaven and keep wondering whether Father has seen through them. . . . They go to bed at night and are not at all sure they will wake up well the next morning. . . . Nothing is one thing only where Divine is concerned. While it is true that retribution represents a medium of effective intimidation to him, it also represents a medium for self-security which he will always need more than most people. . . . It is the knife that he who is, in the last analysis, George Baker, can use against a hostile white world. It is his most vital mechanism for denial of the true status of the Negro in America.*

Divine was vindictive against rival gods, and in Harlem there were several. One of them fell from the sky in a plane. Another fled the country for a time. His most formidable rival was a preacher named Daddy Grace, whose ostentatious virility contrasted with Divine's seemly chastity. (Jim

*Sara Harris and Harriet Crittenden, *Father Divine: Holy Husband* (New York: Doubleday, 1953), pp. 190-91.

Jones also admired Daddy Grace.) Opposed by rival cults and the established churches, Divine held his ground. He had more followers; more people giving him their "all."

He decreed a form of communalism, a sort of coed monasticism, crystallized around the affirmation that when one "has" God, one needs little else. People took on names like Dove of Peace and Sweet Harmony; they exuded rectitude. In return they lived for next to nothing in a Divine dormitory, ate for next to nothing in a Divine restaurant, and worked for next to nothing in a Divine shop, business, or hotel.

Divine himself, however, lived in a splendor befitting godliness. His concerns, apart from remaining omnipotent, were apparently humanitarian and explicitly integrationist. In his residences, sexually segregated as they were, there were ideally two to a bed. But never both black or both white. There was continual testimony to the redemption experienced in Divine's nonracist heaven.

When he was in trouble Divine wrote letters to government officials. His followers wrote as well. When Fiorello LaGuardia came campaigning in Divine's presence, the applause was all for Divine. (When Rosalynn Carter came to a Jones rally, the applause was all for Jones.) In the late 1930s Divine held a convention to which he invited both President and pope. There it was moved, seconded, and unanimously passed that Divine was God. Humanitarian and progressive social measures were advocated: The U. S. should abolish lynching, integrate schools, and pay off the national debt.

Certain of Divine's tenets were bound to cause difficulty. One was that his followers did not die. When one member did expire, Divine ordered everyone else confined to their rooms so that the police could remove the embarrassing evidence of faith's mortality.

Then there was Divine's own mortality. In 1953, otherwise cogent observers predicted mass suicide by

Divine's followers if Divine were to die. But Divine lived twelve more years, into the era of Malcolm X, Watts, and Martin Luther King. At the end, he was perhaps one hundred years old. And when he did die, the suicides did not come. His movement simply declined.

On one level Divine's methods seemed almost, but never quite, comical. When established civil rights organizations were pleading with Metropolitan Life to integrate Manhattan's then new Stuyvesant Gardens, Divine contented himself with a letter to the company president threatening retribution. But Divine enjoined positiveness, affirmation of one's powers and abilities, and rejection of defeatist self-images. He required that all past debts be repaid— debts of all sorts. One of his followers even paid back a social work agency. "I believe in Father Divine. I don't believe in assistances." Another tenet was independence, a fierce insistence on making it on one's own. God gave people the strength to stand on their own two feet. Divine was adamant that there should be no acceptance of gifts or holiday bonuses from employers. Instead, followers were instructed to return gifts with the curt suggestion that their salaries be increased.

The most controversial tenet of Divine's theocracy was his abolition of marriage and sexual relations. This injunction was accepted (sometimes with difficulty) by his followers. They were permitted to lavish their affections on Father Divine, experiencing utter heights of bliss without the complexities of sexual intimacy. To Divine, carnal sex was "a dirty thing," and marriage was a system submitting women to slavery or prostitution. A contemporary observer suggested that the movement would be destroyed if it were thought to be a haven of interracial sex. Divine was married himself but maintained that it was spiritual.

The true believer gained a genuine feeling of warmth and security in Father Divine's presence, a secure living with compatible brothers and sisters, and a chance to pursue a holy life.

The communalism of Father Divine was hardly an ideological response to American capitalism; rather, it was a device to give people who had no stake in the system a sorely needed sense of community control. What was the consolation of a personally owned enterprise if, as part of Divine's kingdom, you could contribute to the growth of an establishment that would ultimately make Divine—already God—the residential neighbor of Franklin Roosevelt? For in truth Divine did obtain a property in Roosevelt's beloved Hyde Park, New York.

Redemption to Father Divine was not merely for the healthy, who had no need of a physician. He dragged from the streets the dregs of society—prostitutes and pimps, thieves and frauds. (So, too, did Jones.) He also healed the hopelessly ill. Within the faithful movement there was testimony always to Father Divine's power to bring lost souls to life.

It appears in retrospect—though Divine's obituaries in the *New York Times* and the New York *Herald Tribune* did not dwell on the subject—that Divine was operating in an almost instinctive manner to give voice to a prophetic protest. It seems that he had a dominant sense that the orderly processes of social evolution were not about to integrate the black domestics and common laborers and welfare recipients who flocked to his banquets into white society. And so he embodied a divine impatience and articulated an integrated community beyond the shabby realities of class and caste. His heavens sprang up full-blown, and his operations were financed by the austerity of the poor and the sacrifice of wealth by members drawn from the privileged classes. Ecstasy was the reward—ecstasy and celebration and immediate joy in the Lord. Here was a redemption that could be touched, felt, and seen, no blatantly hypocritical proclamation of a unity that did not exist. Body to body, bed to bed, table to table—with something approaching tragic dignity—the heavens stood as a kind of testimony to the injustice of society.

The greatest fault of the movement, perhaps, was that children suffered. There was no great premium on the care of the young. Marriage and the human family was, after all, a residue of the world from which the followers were escaping. So followers were sometimes hauled into court for neglect, and the treatment of children became a widespread basis for denigration of the movement. (The death of the Jonestown children may be seen as a reflection that life without Jones was not worth living.)

Father Divine is hard to judge by the standards of nonidolatry, radical tolerance, help to the helpless, and democracy. What seems unusual about Divine was both the justness of his protest and the fact that there is scant evidence that he was corrupted by his power. The movement was idolatrous, but there were "reasons."

In the early 1960s Father Divine received as a visitor a young minister named Jim Jones. Can there be any doubt that many of the central tenets of People's Temple were adaptations of Divine's heavens? No less than eight factors suggest an affirmative conclusion.

1. The focusing of attention on a single spiritual leader.
2. The assertion that all—health, living, a sense of life's mission—would be provided to those who gave up the outside world and cast their lot with the leader.
3. Ecstatic services of worship where there were healings and other miracles.
4. A background of endemic racism that enabled the leader to create an interracial community that stood in contrast to the rest of society.
5. A policy requiring followers to contribute all posses-

sions to the leader's organization, creating considerable economic leverage.

6. Development of a "cult" around the person of the leader—superstitions, images, songs, healing medallions, professions of adoration as a part of common speech.

7. An unwillingness to accept death as a reality. Divine categorically insisted his followers would not die. Prior to the end Jones implied that his members would not die.

8. Considerable rage at defections. Divine moved to Philadelphia permanently rather than pay a modest judgment in favor of a defector who wanted to reclaim property given to the movement. Jones manifested increasing rage at defectors, even though he claimed until the end that followers were free to leave.

But consider also the contrasts:

1. Differing in race and social orientation, Divine was clearly moored in the mentality of the black underclass, having progressive, though not revolutionary, instincts. His home base, the ghetto, accepted what most of white society would regard as outlandish posturing. Jones, by contrast, moved up from lower class obscurity. Thus he had to modify certain of his claims or risk "exposure." In the end, as Jesse Jackson pointed out, Jones was a white leader in whom desperate blacks mistakenly placed their trust. He was "brought down" in part by the efforts of disconcerted middle-class white followers.

2. They differed at the point of a sense of humor. Father Divine spoke of being "combusted" one day at the corner of Lenox and 134th streets in Harlem. Jones appeared to have lacked a sense of humor; he is said to have engaged in sarcastic put-downs and ridicule. Humor is one index of security. Father Divine

manifested a personal serenity, even aplomb, lacking in Jim Jones.

3. Divine practiced absolutism, allowing for a "suspension of disbelief"; Jones did not make absolute claims but required a far more absolutist obedience. Consider Divine's fanciful explanation of his first wife's death, an event which he did not announce (given the fact that death was "forbidden") until he determined to marry a second time.

> God had grown bald on Peninah's [his first wife] account. He had surrounded himself with young virgins because she had requested him to. For these two favors, she heartily thanked him. Now she wanted one more boon. She wished him to take the spirit out of her homely old body and to place it in a young virgin body that would be attractive to his eyes. . . . (Divine's second wife was young, blonde, and Canadian). In all the generations he'd known Peninah, Father had never been able to deny her anything. And, knowing that she was one of the most persistent of angels and would allow him no rest until he met this onerous supplication, he took the beautiful spirit and removed it intact from the homely body in which it had been lodged. In one way, this was the most herculean task Father Divine has ever been called upon to accomplish.*

James Jones shared with white American Protestantism a certain humorlessness and an inability to achieve that legitimate suspension of disbelief which is necessary to open up creative theological—and scientific—discourse. The result was a literalism that led him to use chicken entrails to prove he had extracted cancers from the bowels of persons he had "healed." On the same level, sadly enough, the ruse worked.

*Ibid, pp. 269-70.

4. Divine looked at the outer world with a bemused and generally haughty disdain; Jones looked at the world as space to be conquered, finally as an implacable enemy. Divine sought and desired no self-justification from beyond. Jones became preoccupied with success. He finally had to win a place in history, at all costs.

5. Divine developed a consistent and unchanging theology of self that lasted him over six decades. Jones gave every appearance of having altered his self-understanding to fit times and occasions. The more he claimed to be God, the less he theologized. In the end, he appeared more like a Chinese Communist field commander (in a photograph) than a reverend. (William F. Buckley has even advocated the dropping of "reverend" from Jones's name because the final rejection of religion was so complete.)

6. Divine built "heavens" that were clearly earthbound and hardly utopian; Jones, more and more under fire, tried to build a utopia and called it a socialist heaven. Divine's heavens permitted and encouraged communication with the outside world; Jones's utopia was totally isolated. Divine made a careful success; Jones made an almost inevitable failure.

7. Divine remained aloof from the daily life of his heavens and, over time, insisted that he could be worshiped in spirit from afar. Jones tried to be everywhere and seems to have used spies and other devices to maintain his omniscience and control.

8. Divine maintained a certain, somewhat shaky, continuity with biblical faith; Jones eventually rejected the Bible completely and insisted his followers read socialist tracts.

9. Divine never owned anything. Property was always in the name of his followers, usually in so many

names that perpetual title seemed assured (not to mention frustration of the U. S. Internal Revenue Service). Jones seems to have accumulated in excess of seven million dollars for purposes yet to be disclosed. Some thought he intended to take the money for himself, indeed, that the mass suicide was a prelude to his escape with the money to live out his life in luxury. At one point on the death tape it seems clear that he wants the flock to die but that he might be willing to live to face the torments he imagines will come. In other words, he really seems to regard death as the better portion.

10. Divine never shared power. He bore the responsibility of being God manfully, as it were. Jones was dependent on various persons throughout his entire career—his wife; the Stoens; and, later, a cadre of counsellors and what appeared to be almost a Red Guard to assist him in the execution of duties. How much was Jones's leadership; how much was commune politics? That remains to be fathomed from the testimony of surviving members.

Jones's failure can be traced as much to his devaluation of himself as to his megalomania. His godliness was a ruse. The evidence is everywhere; in the plethora of pills revealing a hypochondria of mammoth proportions, in his confused yet lethal reaction to the probable murder by his lieutenants of the investigators, in the sickening mad schoolroom atmosphere of the coerced suicides. He summoned the obedient and spoke to them in the tones of a paranoid teacher: Die with dignity! Amid objections and sentimental moments, he struggled to keep the death lines moving. It was a grisly anticommunion.

Hardly the story of a god worth the name. And certainly a departure from the five-foot god who may have once inspired him to see the advantages inherent in the business of religion.

CHAPTER SIX

Healing

How can Satan cast out Satan? If a kingdom is divided against itself, that kingdom cannot stand. And if a house is divided against itself, that house will not be able to stand. And if Satan has risen up against himself and is divided, he cannot stand, *but is coming to an end.**

Not to take Jesus' healing ministry with utmost seriousness is to deny rather than affirm a truly social gospel. Jesus, one might say, pioneers a holistic view of health. It is nothing less than the whole self, the whole "I" that is involved, the ecosystem of the person.

Compare aspects of Jesus' healing ministry with distortion, sham, and cruelty that passed for healing in the People's Temple. The biblical narrative of the house divided against itself is a good explanation for the fate of all evil, especially for the evil that gradually enveloped People's Temple.

There was a progressive aspect in Jesus' healing.

1. Jesus' healing was usually *incidental*. Major points of healing narratives have to do with the being and teaching of Jesus, not with the techniques of healing.

2. No healing takes place for purposes of self-aggrandizement or to win followers or to impress or prove

*Italics added.

himself. Jesus was sought out; he did not advertise. Frequently he enjoined silence following a healing. His healings had profound public impact, but Jesus saw them as a natural part of his ministry.

3. Healings represented a beginning step in a fourfold campaign whereby Jesus revolutionized, even obliterated, the messianic ideal and ushered in a participatory faith based on the premise that human beings may function as forgiving moral agents in the world. The sign of this premise is the working of the Holy Spirit, the awakening to a realized life. The other three steps in Jesus' campaign were his teaching, his social ministry, and his handling of the conflict that led to his last days.

If one takes seriously the initials A.D. (in the year of the Lord), believing that the gospel story is a true turning point of time as well as an indication of our successes and failures to embody its principles of participatory democracy, radical tolerance, and alliance of the privileged with the helpless on a voluntary basis; one may describe the gospel, in Jacques Maritain's felicitous words, as an "evangelical ferment" within civilization. During World War II, Maritain wrote:

If the ever-growing schism between the true behavior of our world and the moral and spiritual principles on which its firmness depended were to bring about a final rupture in balance, if our world has little by little been emptied of its spirit, and has seemed at length a universe of words, an unleavened mass, if the catastrophe has become inevitable, the tremendous historical fund of energy and truth accumulated for centuries is still available to human freedom, the forces of renewal are on the alert and it is still up to us to make sure that this catastrophe of the modern world is not a regression to a perverted aping of the Ancient Regime or of the Middle Ages, and that it does not wind up in the totalitarian putrefaction of the German New Order. It is up to us to see that it merges in a new and truly creative age, where [we] in suffering and hope will resume [our] journey toward the conquest of freedom.*

Jesus' healing contains a regenerative power for the Body Social as well as for the individual. Maritain makes us conscious of the need to Christianize our social impulses. He emphasizes our obligations to history. We have many, many divisions of our own to heal: the fissures between religion and science, science and art. It is only too plain that we ignore these fissures at our peril. We cannot preserve health without inner unity and vision, and Jonestown is a grim parody: the ultimate unity of the dead.

Before moving his congregation from Redwood Valley to San Francisco, Jones made his presence known not as a social prophet but as a healer. In Redwood Valley he had amassed a fleet of eleven used Greyhound buses to transport his flock to the city on weekends. He would rent a hall, and there he would heal. Kilduff and Javers report that Jones blanketed the city's Fillmore and Bayview neighborhoods with flyers like the following, which they quote:

PASTOR JAMES JONES . . . Incredible! Miraculous! Amazing!
. . . The Most Unique Prophetic Healing Service You've Ever Witnessed! Behold the Word Made Incarnate in Your Midst!
—God works as tumorous masses are passed in every service
. . . Before your eyes, the crippled walk, the blind see!
—Scores are called out of the audience in each service and told the intimate (but never embarrassing) details of their lives only God could reveal!
—Christ is made real through the most precise revelations and miraculous healings in this ministry of his servant, Jim Jones!
—This same spiritual healing ministry does not oppose medical science in any way. In fact, it is insisted that all regular

*Jacques Maritain, tr. Doris C. Anson, *Christianity and Democracy* (New York: Arno, 1944), pp. 23-24.

members have yearly medical examinations and co-operate fully with their physicians.

—See God's Supra-Natural Works Now!*

Many people sincerely professed to have been cured by Jones's ministrations. Perhaps, in the intense emotionalism generated by the services, healings did occur. There were others, however, who sought to expose Jones's rank charlatanism. Curious journalists tended to focus on the healings. In September 1972, Lester Kinsolving, a religious writer for the *San Francisco Examiner*, produced a critical column noting two main facts about Jones's operation.

1. Jones publicly claimed to have raised forty persons from the dead, "people stiff as a board, tongues hanging out, eyes set, skin graying and all vital signs absent."

2. Jones had a retinue of aides obviously armed with pistols and guns, whose ostensible purpose was to protect their leader in the face of various "threats."

To these facts Kinsolving added a picture of Jones as "darkly handsome . . . clad in a white turtleneck sweater, a pulpit gown and dark glasses . . . seated on a cushion-covered stool behind the podium—which is an important necessity, given the five- and six-hour length of his services."

Jones, in a subsequent *Examiner* interview, claimed that forty-three had indeed been raised from the dead, that there had not been a failure ("No one has died."), and that all the "resurrections" took place inside the church. The Kinsolving critique, incidentally, evoked two days of picketing outside the *Examiner* offices by Jones's followers.

Healing had its limits. Those who knew the Guyana situation claimed that nutrition there was minimal in

*Marshall Kilduff and Ron Javers, *Suicide Cult* (New York, 1978).

protein, hardly enough to sustain an adequate level of health in a utopian commune.

According to ex-members and defectors, the primary purpose of the "healing services" was to impress outsiders so they would join the fold. Jones used the fluctuations of his own health as a means of controlling people. Faith was not a conspicuous mode by which he dealt with his own illnesses. Pills seem to have been the major device.

Jones knew how to confront people with what they most feared. One story capturing the pathos of Jonestown concerned Mrs. Lisa Phillips Layton. It was told to the *New York Times* on December 4, 1977, in detail, and represents a valuable contribution to understanding the complex reasons that people felt committed to the People's Temple. Mrs. Layton joined the congregation after she became convinced of the cure of her brother-in-law, allegedly ill with cancer. It was reported that he *thought* he had cancer; he didn't know for sure. Mrs. Layton joined, turning over some $250,000 to People's Temple. During 1977 she became ill and learned that she had cancer. "Mr. Jones," reported the *New York Times*, "repeatedly sent word that he could cure from Guyana, and she waited for his efforts to work." The account continues:

> But finally her cancer became so advanced that it was necessary for surgeons to remove a lung.
>
> Deborah and Larry Layton (two of her children) were still with Mr. Jones at that point, having remained as key lieutenants even after his doctrine of good works and selflessness had begun to become an increasingly paranoid self-adulation.
>
> "Jim could really get to people," Deborah recalled in an interview. "He'd work you so hard you didn't have time to complain, and he'd blackmail you; he destroyed marriages and humiliated you."
>
> After her operation, Mrs. Layton moved to Guyana. Initially she was allowed to recuperate in a cabin of her own (there), but

later she was moved into a crowded dormitory-style cabin crowded with other elderly women. Deborah nursed her mother and tried to conceal her discovery from a physician that the cancer was fatal. Mr. Jones, Deborah said, callously gave Mrs. Layton that news.

When Jones claimed to be God, when he threw the Bible across the room and cried out that people should listen to him instead, he reportedly told a follower, "Worship me, and I'll back it up with miracles."

The picture of the fall in Genesis may be considered a legend. But it is a legend, as Kierkegaard says in *The Concept of Dread*, "representing as outward that which occurs inwardly." In this work Kierkegaard details several telltale signs of the "demoniacal," which he terms "dread of the good." One of the signs is "shut-upness . . . the fact that unfreedom makes a prisoner precisely of itself." A second aspect is *"the sudden"*—another word for this, perhaps closer to modern experience of dictators, is the *arbitrary*. The demoniacal is a transgression of limits—exactly because, to the demoniac, there are *no* limits. "Unfreedom makes a prisoner precisely of itself." Jones's throwing the Bible across the room is, in Kierkegaardian terms, a true picture of demoniacal action: the suddenness of it, the unexpectedness of it. One is lulled into a sense of security and trust, then, an action occurs to freeze one's blood. Experiences such as these are not infrequent in the testimony of those who knew Jones.

Simone Weil has aptly said, "The criterion for those things which come from God is that they show all the characteristics of madness except for the loss of capacity to discern truth and love justice." And yet Jonestown clouded the issue in a Hartford Theological Seminary classroom. A week after Jonestown, there was a discussion of healing ministries. Students considered how they might, in the local setting, develop their own healing practices. After Jonestown, not one person in the class was willing even to discuss it! Jim Jones had cast a shadow on the healing possibilities of the church. The class seemed paralyzed.

There is a healing that must take place following Jonestown, not a fearful assertion that "we" are not "them," that "our" church is not "their" church. Jesus emphasizes that the worst thing we can do is to deny the power of the Holy Spirit. Jesus teaches us to have faith in the Spirit's workings. Let us, despite the horror of Jonestown, move closer to the realms of existence where the Spirit operates and is welcome. We need to affirm the growing effort to bring the narrative power of scripture to bear on the healing of the person through the medium of storytelling; a continuing humanistic attempt to appropriate the discoveries of science within an integrated scheme of health that bespeaks wholeness; the growth of noncoercive healing ministries that evidence sensitivity toward conditions that can be affected but not fundamentally changed; and whatever movement there might be to cultivate the practice of prayer as advocated by Jesus, prayer that finally rests on faith in the one who calls Jesus beloved, prayer that can say, in the heart of despair, "Not my will, but thine, be done."

CHAPTER SEVEN

The Responsible Self

IN AN APOCALYPTIC age such as ours, it is not surprising that a person with no strong mooring in faith will escape into spiritual mystique or grasp the coattails of a charismatic leader. It becomes increasingly difficult to define precisely the nature of coercion, of manipulative criminality. And amid the general confusion, people look toward the state to solve the crisis.

The warning signals that might have averted the tragedy of Jonestown were suppressed, ignored, or camouflaged. When things in Jonestown reached the point of beatings, unscrupulous practices, and suicide threats, it was too late. In desperation, relatives of people in Guyana went to the state, to Congressman Leo Ryan, to get a sympathetic hearing.

Ryan, who had cultivated a reputation as an unorthodox champion of schoolchildren and prisoners, now chose to come to the aid of petrified supplicants who saw death waiting in the wings. Nothing could be better designed to bring public rage to bear against the state for failing to suppress the cult. The rage was not directed at Ryan, who died in the cause of liberating Jonestown defectors, but against various government agencies for failing to act on prior indications that the People's Temple was headed for disaster.

Quite apart from the defensible rights of any religious institution under the First Amendment, one wonders what the government could have done to suppress a leader who controlled the minds and allegiance of a vast majority of his followers, who delivered nightly perorations against the government, and who conducted suicide drills in order to test his followers' loyalty and prepare them for the Armageddon festering in his mind. It has been alleged that Sirhan Sirhan came under the influence of a particularly nefarious cult called the Process. Lee Arthur Bremer's diaries open up a world of delusion that might have been perceived by some before he sought to blast George Wallace off the face of the earth. Squeaky Fromme, would-be vanguard of the Manson assassination effort, was said to be brainwashed. Could any of these have been prevented by more government intervention?

Unless there is to be total surveillance on the part of the state, individuals must themselves assert authority over their own lives. And communities must be aware of the ebbs and flows that determine the quality of life. Religious institutions could well see in Jonestown a clarion call, not demanding of the state a proxy conscience, not retreating to a defensive posture of claiming independence under the Constitution. They could see Jonestown instead as a springboard to consider the very basis of their faith. It is my conviction that a valid quest of this sort and much serious reflection would move religious institutions toward a discussion of how they may, in all validity, exercise an effect upon their own constituencies and on the public at large. For at the heart of a response to Jonestown lies not a cry of "What can the state do?" but "What can *we* do to affirm, nurture, and bring into being the responsible self?"

Biblical faith points to the conscious self as the most precious entity there is and to freedom as the most precious fruit of consciousness. This assumption is founded on the belief that the individual is a moral agent, a belief that has been steadily eroding in our time. One might cite here the past unwillingness of science to engage in a discussion of values on the basis that such intangibles are "nonverifiable." Study of the works of Thomas Szatz will make one aware of the threats to the integrity of the individual as moral agent that arise from psychoanalytic jargon, the tendency to call evil a "sickness." Yet it is only on the basis of the moral self that freedom can have meaning. All reflection concerning the state, the role of the judicial system, institutions, and the family hinge on the affirmation of the ultimate value of the self.

The self is in some ways similar to our ideas of the cell. The cell has a wall, not an impenetrable shell but a porous wall through which various substances can pass. To the extent that the porous, flexible wall of the cell is bruised or damaged, even shattered, the interior (the self, in this analogy) is made vulnerable. The act of enabling a helpless person—a child, for example—to grow and flourish does not involve breaking down the wall but affirming its existence, guarding a precious individuality that must not be violated. To break the wall, to impugn what lies behind it, to appropriate that inner realm of freedom and individuality for one's own uses, to see it as a territory to be invaded, is to create a reciprocal sickness. Life-preserving autonomy gives way to potentially demonic enslavement. Inevitably, the invader is one whose own cell wall has deteriorated, one who knows not who or what he or she is and thus must feed upon another. The relationship between charismatic leader and obedient follower is a mutual eating away of selfhood.

In the wake of Jonestown some of my New England friends remarked that they had been thrust farther into a Thoreaulike individualism. And I felt much the same way. And yet Alexis de Tocqueville averred that the opportunity and also the danger of a democratic society such as ours lies in the possible atomization of individuals, the tendency for people to be so thrust upon their own resources that ultimately they are not able to bear their own freedom. The solution lies in some correct balance between selfhood and society.

It is characteristic of our time that we are confused not only about the self but also about what constitutes a proper mode of relationship among selves. This is not a new confusion. It is part of life's pilgrimage in every age. But today we are faced with formidable challenges, threats that could empty the self of its inner space, its inner sphere of validity. Meditation is a partial antidote to this tendency, largely ignored by established religion. To empty the self of its inner space is to imperil its sense of freedom. Perhaps this explains, at least in part, the popularity of B.F. Skinner's ideas. How much does a theory that a human person operates like a conditioned mechanism appeal to people who have no very strong sense of their own freedom?

Freedom tends to disappear under the harsh lights of the laboratory. The crisis of the individual, which is in the widest sense a crisis in human history, is not letting up; but, on the contrary, it is deepening in the face of the growing arsenal of controls which can, and sometimes do, reach terrifying levels of capacity to tear down the walls and shatter the self.

Emphasis on consciousness, conscience, freedom, the soul, and the self alone will not solve social problems that result from lack of education, employment, or ecological consideration. But the destruction of the self is mainly what Jonestown was about.

Post-Jonestown reflection throws into question a frequent nostrum advanced by those who write about improving society, who say that the enemy of change in American life is rampant individualism. Only by modifying individualism, they claim, can there be greater harmony and cohesion in society. But individualism hardly seems the dominant culprit in a society that became, in the 1970s, a seedbed of cults that have the explicit goal of breaking down individuals to the point that they can fit into the group with the least amount of friction. The fund of individualism within our society is one of the most precious commodities we have. It is hardly rampant.

Consider a community known throughout history for its forceful—often abrasive—individualism; its incredible flights of artistry and thought and, at the same time, its close-knit solidarity. From time immemorial the Jews have stood in testimony to the reciprocity that exists between an almost jealous regard for the self and a passionate regard for the community. There is an enduring correlation between community and self, and it instinctively abhors the notion of a self-worshiping charismatic leader. Leanings toward idolatry are vigorously excoriated by the prophets and the prophetic tradition, which has served Israel well over millennia, guarding self and community and maintaining proper balance between them. This heritage lives not by ideology, which often reduces the person to the level of a "social unit," but according to two ancient formulas. The first is the Shema Israel: "Hear, O Israel, the Lord thy God is one God." The second is the Jeremiad, the Old Testament prophetic message of which Jesus is the ultimate expression.

The Jeremiad is the calling of the human community to a moral accounting. It summons us to remember the moral roots of society. It is these roots that form the basis of civilization and history. The Jeremiad never counsels complete withdrawal into a world of contemplative stasis. It always assumes a possibility of social progress, of advance, despite moral lapses and failures. To the extent that the charter of selfhood embodied in the original moral law is transgressed, to the extent that there is a social demoralization and confusion, the Jeremiad goes farther than remembrance and hope. It embraces the need of each individual self for new birth.

A philosophy of life that takes freedom seriously will take the Jeremiad seriously. It is the element of religious and social ethic that cries out of the memory, pain, and hope of the beleaguered human spirit. It cries out to God in desolation, "As the hart longs for the living stream, so longs my soul for thee!"

The Jeremiad is a bridge between the individual and the communal search. Jonestown may be able to produce a little good, if bitter, fruit if it shocks us into a frame of mind similar to that evoked by the Jeremiad: imaginative and clear thinking and, at the same time, an awareness of what is involved in the spiritual leap humanity must take if it is indeed to move into the Third Millennium A.D. with faith, and hope, and love.

We need no further obliteration of the self, no further denigration of the reality of moral conscience. We need, instead, an affirmation of responsible selfhood. Only then can we speak meaningfully of the common values by which we might live as a people.

CHAPTER EIGHT

The Democratization of Messianism

THE PSYCHOTHERAPIST JAY HALEY wrote an essay entitled, "The Power Tactics of Jesus Christ."* Jesus' skills, he suggested, are those of power politics, which we can only now begin to appreciate, thanks to the disappearance of Christianity as a real religious force. While I do not agree with these assumptions, I do believe they constitute a formidable and seductive challenge to a balanced biblical faith. And a rationale for what might otherwise appear a ludicrous contrast between Jesus and Jim Jones.

According to Haley, Jesus organized a movement that prefigured the mass movements of the modern period. The power tactics of Jesus have informed or inspired movements of even those who discredited him: Lenin, Trotsky, Hitler, Mussolini, Mao, Ho Chi Minh, Castro, Elijah Mohammed. Jesus is the author of the ruling notion of mass movements: that organization be carried out among the dispossessed and that the movement exist outside the dominant power structure thus functioning to undermine the adversary.

*Jay Haley, *The Power Tactics of Jesus Christ and Other Essays* (New York: Avon Books, 1969).

Haley traced through the Gospels the development of Jesus as a political genius whose goal was allegedly the formation of a movement that could topple established power. It is interesting to compare Haley's observations about Jesus with what is known about Jim Jones:

1. Jesus entered the religious arena as an unknown faced with a formidable power structure.
2. Jesus lived at a time when common folk belief was that a single person could set things right.
3. The easiest way to become known within a short time was to become a religious prophet, goading the establishment but always couching criticisms in the context of the tradition in order to show the hypocrisy of the ruling powers.
4. Healing was the means Jesus used to spread his name throughout the land. His reticence about his achievements was gratuitous, since anyone who is healed will spread the healer's fame automatically. According to Haley, acts of healing tend to raise people's expectations and encourage "wishful thinking."
5. Audacious attacks upon the religious establishment increased the popular attraction of Jesus.
6. Jesus deviated from prophetic tradition by seeking to build an organization around his goals. He built an elite, said to number seventy persons. He drew from dispossessed groups and asked common people to give up everything to go with him.
7. He tied followers to him with promises of future bliss. He kept followers unsteady by vacillating on his promises.
8. He assumed there would be persecution.
9. He proclaimed the right of the downtrodden to rule and coupled this with scathing criticisms of the rich.
10. Jesus' kingdom of God promised that the humiliated

would reign. To this Haley compares Hitler's thousand-year Reich and Marx's classless society.

11. Jesus' insistence that he spoke for "the Father" was typically revolutionary; he developed faith in a distant ideal, at the same time claiming to be the only true interpreter of that ideal.
12. The major contribution of Jesus to the development of power tactics was his adaptation of the animal strategem of "surrender." A dog can disarm an attacking dog by presenting its exposed throat for the kill and thereby incapacitating the "victor." To turn the other cheek is a profound form of aggressive power in a battle between unequals.
13. Haley further suggests that the tactics of meekness are most effective when supported by vague threats of violent uprising, as during the civil rights movement of the 1960s.
14. Jesus' attack on the money changers was a stroke of tactical genius because he hit opponents at their weakest point. He clearly intended to be arrested, according to Haley.
15. After his arrest Jesus did not intend to die. In most accounts he acted, says Haley, to avoid condemnation. His final execution resulted from a miscalculation, a failure to read the opposition properly. Even the best tacticians fail.

Haley's thesis is one-dimensional. It also demonstrates the limitations of a purely "biblical narrative" approach. It is one reason why it is needful to arrive at a value system which itself can serve as a corrective to distortions in the telling. But apart from this, there are at least three historical problems with Haley's version of the story.

1. Christianity could as easily be seen as a religious weapon of the ruling classes as of the oppressed.

There is within the New Testament ample basis for assuming that a hierarchical status quo should be maintained, that slaves should not be freed. Thus Augustine accepts the misery of the lowest classes as their just deserts. And by and large the Protestant reformers, reading Paul selectively, side with the nobility against the peasantry. Such an approach is as much a distortion as Haley's, but the reason for the diversity of readings lies partly in the biblical narrative itself.

2. In the modern era the world's established churches are predominantly *middle* class in outlook. They have tended to encourage a middle-class ethos of social redemption, as Max Weber and others have observed. The middle class is not inevitably reactionary, but it is not Haley's "oppressed."

3. Until recently, the religion of the poor and dispossessed has been otherworldly; biblical stories have been read as allegories of redemption beyond time and space, not as concrete indications for change in the here and now.

Today there is major debate within upper- and middle-class religion about social priorities, human rights, economic responsibility, and styles of living. At the same time there is an almost geological shift among the once otherworldly or socially passive lower-class faiths toward more immediate social goals. We are set today for a portentous convergence of these two tendencies, a meeting of streams that can vastly alter the coming course of religious attitudes. The most obvious goal of underclass aspiration is entrance into the world of the middle class. And the middle class shows at least some degree of unrest about the values inherent in the pursuit of material goods and the acceptance of a depersonalized structure of work and services. This is a paradox that we need to ponder and to understand. It is a double movement toward a potentially nonviolent economic and cultural revolution.

A consideration of the last days of Jesus serves to further underline the one-dimensionality in Haley's argument.

1. *How are we to perceive Jesus' journey to Jerusalem?* This journey was not taken to precipitate merely the political crisis of the moment but to initiate a cosmic break. Its purpose was to live out Jesus' task as the inaugurator of a new era in history, in which the revelation of universal redemption was to be spread over the entire world. For this reason the confrontation was with the religious authorities and only secondarily with the state. In Jerusalem, Jesus turned over the tables of the money changers, declaring that the temple is meant to be the house of prayer for *all* nations. A religious challenge!
   Also, Jesus was hardly able to collect a tightly knit revolutionary band. On the contrary, there is the continual sense that even his closest disciples were mystified by Jesus. Very few were able to understand the nature of the being with whom they were dealing.

2. *How does the betrayal by Judas fit into the story?* The betrayal by Judas may be explained as a crisis of messianic expectation, a crisis on the level of local politics. Judas represented zealous political concern within the circle of Jesus. He was no doubt an ardent critic of Jesus' "wastefulness" when Jesus let a woman anoint him with precious oil. The money could have been spent to help the poor! One can see Judas as a manifestation of Herculean conscience, akin to Dostoevski's portrayal of the political idealist whose end is suicide because he cannot grasp the power of faith and the Holy Spirit to accomplish what politics, apart from responsible selfhood, cannot do.

103

3. *Is the crucifixion, then, a necessary stage of Jesus'
   announcement of a new age?* Yes. It was necessary that
   he suffer even the forsaking of himself by the One he
   called Father in order to vanquish the enemies of the
   new age, the powers of the demons and of death
   itself. The goal was transphysical, that is to say,
   spiritual. This was shown in several ways. The
   disciples were confused and fearful of arrest. They
   deserted him; they did not comprehend what was
   taking place. Even Nature itself shuddered at the
   death that took place at Golgotha. Whether one
   wishes to read this as myth or not, no clearer picture
   could be given of the breaking of the divine into
   human history. One could call it a release into the
   world of a substance of higher potency, though
   "substance" may not be quite the word to express the
   subsequent coming of the Holy Spirit at Pentecost.
   Again and again, one comes to the root tenet of the
   faith, expressed in the central images of the story: that
   human history is not a horizontal, one-dimensional
   affair. The cross expresses not only the form of the
   human body but also the form of history. The coming
   of the Holy Spirit is a continuation of the mission of
   Jesus. All humanity is thus called and enabled to enter
   into the work of justice and love.
4. *What is the significance of the Last Supper?* It is primarily a
   remembrance. It suggests that a span of time must
   elapse as the world moves toward redemption. It
   remembers the vision of a new age and affirms our
   capacity to live and deepen the freedom implied in
   Jesus' teachings.

Biblical faith is a direct negation of the conventional
messianic notion of a single person functioning as deliverer
of the group, of the supernatural (as opposed to historical)
appearance of a golden age. And yet if one is candid about

modern revolutionary movements, they *have* coalesced around messianic leaders; they *have* set themselves up as bearers of a standard of liberation against the fortress of the oppressors; they *have* operated on a Manichaean notion of good and evil that is, in its way, a mirror image of the hostility and fear that goads the powerful oppressor to punitive measures.

And who is to say that the hour in which traditional religion, particularly that of the established powers, can proclaim a universally valid system of values—essentially a democratization of the messianic ideal—is not either long since past or irretrievably in the future? This seems to be the underlying apocalyptic assumption of the editors of the London *Economist*, who pondered Jonestown in the following observation.

One by one the secular heroes of the past century—Lenin, Stalin, Mao, even Marx himself—have begun to lose their appeal. Instead, a groping has begun for new forms of spiritual experience. The cults and sects and communities which are looking for new ideas in this field are the most numerous in the United States because America is, in this matter too, 20 years ahead of the rest of the world. . . . The grass has begun to force itself through the cracks in the agnostic concrete.

It is a period of experimentation; and, like all such periods, it is disorderly, hopeful and terrifying. Anything goes. Elements of Christianity mix in with elements of the old Eastern religions and philosophies. Half-forgotten fragments of animism, and of the dark other side of the religious coin, are taken up and tried out. . . . It could take well into the twenty-first century before all these experiments finally take shape as coherent new bodies of spiritual belief, with coherent new institutions to run them.

If things go well, the time between now and then could prove to be as important in the development of human consciousness as, say . . . the first century of the Christian era (which saw the offering of a new link between the spiritual and material halves of life). . . . It could—if things go well—lead to a reconciliation of the thinking, scientific, part of the human mind with the feeling, instinctive part under the command of conscious will: a pacification of the long civil war in inner space.

The reconciliation of the long civil war in inner space, the truce between conscience and aggression, will not be won by cults or messianic religious or political movements. Such movements are symptoms of division and economic and spiritual malaise, not the cure. Communities built around biblical faith and the gospel narrative may be best suited to carry out the task of midwifing a step in consciousness during the coming decades. There is a reason for this beyond those previously advanced: The freedom that biblical faith proclaims is based on something very different from the freedom to which messianic movements aspire. It is based on the assurance that humanity's most embarrassing need is indeed fulfilled. That is the constant need for forgiveness, a confirmation that at the deepest level we are accepted. Science fiction, which recognizes the possibility of cosmic disaster, is a good mirror of the future. There are moments in science fiction when, in some arid future time as persons search for signs amid the rubble, the surviving human word that will not be obliterated is the ancient *kyrie eleison*: Lord have mercy! Christ have mercy! It is the incomparable capacity of biblical faith to balance the demands of accommodation to the inbreaking realm of redemption, with the continuing need for forgiveness that gives its institutions not only the hope but the mandate to survive.

The signs have been with us for a century and more. They are the manifold indications that we are called to enworld the faith. There have been myriad false starts. Political revolutions have made a mockery of tolerance and democracy. Religious groups have fought tooth and nail merely to preserve an institutional hegemony. But the signs that are most propitious are those which point to the messianic wreckage of our century and say, "No! No! This is not the way."

To enworld the faith is not to reduce its richness but to enrich the world with the variety of its nuances. It is to flood the world not with coercive creeds but with wise tellers of tales. It is to move beyond *us* and *them* to a positive recognition of the presence of the Spirit wherever the Spirit chooses to be. We have not witnessed the failure of the enworlding process. We have witnessed false starts and tragic distortions. Who will say that now is not a propitious moment for a new advance, a reconciliation, a seeing once again of God's promise—the rainbow—beyond the one-dimensionality of Haley's thesis?

CHAPTER NINE

Toward a New Classification of Religious Institutions

C*onfusion in the* wake of Jonestown was intensified by the relative inadequacy of terms applied to various religious organizations to explain various differences between them. Possibly a rush to attain journalistic insights accounted for the indiscriminate lumping together of everything from the Manson family to the peaceful Sufis under the ominous heading of cult. Apart from such invidious classification, the grim aftermath of Jonestown beckons us to evaluate religious groups with reference to the values that underlie their behavior.

The difficulty with traditional classification stems in part from the present inadequacy of the terms church, sect, and cult. None conveys a clear meaning today. Church will always be an ambiguous term because it can imply various institutional forms and belief systems. How are we to comprehend Quakers and Catholics, the local congregation and the denomination, the Pentecostals and the Episcopalians under the name church?

The term sect has often been used as a foil to the word

church—the sect is seen as pure, dogmatic, and antisocial; and the church is seen as fallible, open, compromising, and established. Given the traditional typology and the sped-up nature of contemporary life and movement, it would be possible today for a person to be involved in a church and a sect simultaneously, alternatively, or successively.

Cult also fails to convey much about the character and content of a religious community. We need a new system of classification.

The best alternative to traditional terminology is a value-related typology that defines the nature of religious organization in terms of adherence or nonadherence to certain key concepts.

There is, possibly, a single term that applies to all religious enterprise: *faith*. Churches, sects, and cults alike operate on the basis of various world views, doctrines, and revelations that require that measure of assent we call faith.

1. Some will be *institutional faiths* with a legal entity, a polity, public worship, educational programs, social services, etc.
2. Others will have the character of *intentional faiths*. They will emphasize a high degree of commitment; often a sacrifice of wealth or status; a primary loyalty to the institution and its goals; and a chance to love, witness, and serve with other adherents. Intentional faith implies a degree of free assent within the membership.
3. Others will be *insular faiths*. These will be physically, socially, and by conviction "separate" from both the world and from significant contact with other faiths. They are authoritarian in structure, and there is in their teaching a sense that membership implies "election" to salvation and that this salvation is denied to nonmembers. Such faiths may proselytize

actively, or they may withdraw. But there is about them an aspect of drivenness, a sense that members are not merely giving free assent but are committing large areas of self to an authority system that is dominant and that radically confines autonomy.

Some of the implication of traditional typology survives in the terms institutional, intentional, and insular. There are many churches—particularly those where superstition plays a major part in the belief system ("I gave my will to God, and he led me to do this.")—that could be seen as insular, a few which could be seen as intentional, and others combining elements of all three faith types.

If faith-typing is adequate as a general mode of classification, the addition of a value system by which to evaluate each type is the next step toward an alternative mode of typology. The value system advanced in this essay is implicit—I believe—in biblical understanding. Hardly free from the various modifying social and historical contexts, there is, nevertheless, an inherent authority in the values suggested. But it must be stressed that they be taken as a unity, a dynamic whole, with each correcting the other. When there are severe conflicts between them, it can be shown that there results personal and historical crises of great magnitude. But there will always be *some* conflict. Here, then, are the values:

1. *Nonidolatry.* Expressed positively as giving priority to God, but equally relevant as a denial of priority to anything or anyone else.
2. *Radical tolerance.* The acceptance of divergent views, lifestyles, of the inevitability of diversity.
3. *Aiding the helpless.* Aid to children and all others rendered helpless in any way.
4. *Valuing the democratic process.*

No less important than the stating of these positive values is the articulation of values that are in fundamental tension but that are clearly operative, thus part of the human condition.

1. *Idolatries.* Ascription of supreme value to status, wealth, a particular leader, an abstract idea, a job, work—and anything else that can transgress the worth implied both in tolerance and in the call to the work of enabling the helpless.
2. *Exclusiveness.* Patriarchy, racial purity, order, etc.
3. *"Strength."* Rugged individualism, exclusivistic social ideology, hoarding, institutional- and self-aggrandizement, "security," etc.
4. *Centralization.* Expertise, autocracy, authoritarianism, discouragement of democratic participation.

By subjecting institutions of faith to the series of questions implied by affirmation of a basic value system, it is possible to develop a quite useful mode of evaluation. I have avoided specific suggestions as to how such a system might be charted or otherwise "systematized." The schema is not a basis for the "scientific" classification of religious groups. What is probable is that existing religious groups could undergo a certain self-evaluation in terms of their operating values. It is also quite clear that a value analysis and description of various "cults" would provide a much fairer way of classifying them than at present. Merely because a faith has the marks of insularity, for example, it does not follow that it is inherently idolatrous (of a single leader) or opposed to democratic processes, etc.

What might most help in the classification of religious groups today would be far more support of independent religious journalism than now exists. If any major independent religious journal had done a thorough report on People's Temple, it would have had far more influence on powers that could have intervened than secular

111

journalism did. I can say out of a decade of experience as such a reporter that the amount of time and the resources needed to do a competent beginning story on any organization are equivalent, at minimum, of compensation for up to two months' work. It is doubtful that academics and others without specific journalistic abilities are able to dig out the essential facts and nuances that make competent evaluation possible.

Had People's Temple been evaluated according to the criteria I have advanced, stress would have been far less on the "sincerity" of members (a conspicuous attribute of "cult" people) than on such fundamental questions as, Who is the object of worship? What is the place of the Bible? Are the governing processes democratic? None of these questions would have elicited affirmative results in the case of People's Temple. Therefore it would have been possible to raise severe questions at a relatively early date. Ultimately every value I have advanced was contravened by People's Temple.

How, we might ask, does the value system of those who gathered around Jesus relate to the suggested criteria? The disciples practiced an intentional faith—that is clear. They were consistently warned against idolatry and called to the work of enablement. They were likewise called to respond to the needs of the helpless. Even though Jesus observed that he would be betrayed by one "defector," he made no effort to keep Judas in the ranks. The disciples seemed free to come and go. Indeed, after Jonestown, one of my first thoughts was that perhaps the most healthy aspect of Christianity is that Peter at the crucial moment denied Jesus three times. Hardly what you would call a submissive fanaticism! The teaching of Jesus is laced through with the injunction not to judge. Ultimately the underlying doctrine of forgiveness is the most radical form of the tolerance that he preached.

The reflections in this chapter suggest a general effort to assess the quality of life in today's religious institutions in terms of values. Insofar as such institutions are self-aggrandizing, they violate the spirit of a biblical value system. Insofar as clergy and other leaders are deified, there is a potentially fatal idolatry at work. Insofar as any religious body becomes preoccupied with a finite ethical issue and expends massive energy taking a "moral stand," it may well contravene the word of one who cried out, "Let the one who is without sin cast the first stone." To the extent that a concern for the helpless in every conceivable category is not at the forefront, religious institutions risk exchanging a providential gift—values for life—for a mess of institutional pottage. The system of values propounded here asks any religious institution a series of questions that will tell more about it than an expensive "self-study"; for the values get to the root motivations, the gut responses.

One question is, how seriously do you take the needs of children and, by extension, others who are without help and thus dependent? This question should not raise up a desire to dominate and control the helpless by becoming the paternal (or maternal) "source" of all well-being but, rather, encourage operating in every area with awareness that nothing is more important than that a child be given the resources he or she needs to grow toward responsible adulthood. By seeing the question in this way, all talk of sex and marriage becomes transformed. The widely proclaimed values of adult self-fulfillment are set against the primacy of concern for the child. The value of the child becomes a basis for social planning, economic policy, and discussions of human relationship.

How much weight is put on tolerance? Tolerance of lifestyles that threaten. Tolerance of those who are angry. Tolerance of the outside observer, even the investigator.

How ready are we to give up dull useless abstractions about justice and opposing social systems for a concrete

113

consideration of the condition of children under all systems? Simplistic? It is simplistic only if one fails to see the implication of this approach. The implication is that there is a special role for institutions of faith in the sociopolitical realm—the role of the one who points beyond the conflicts to the actual *effects* of war and starvation and material consumption. Jesus said that it was by the simplicity and foolishness of the logic of the kingdom that we were in fact saved from the snares of this world. A genuine emphasis on the moral precedence of the helpless over values of security and "power" during coming decades will bring religious institutions into a vital relationship with the world as the announcer of imperishable values. This can help create a basis for tough decision-making in the political realm for responsible citizenship by people of faith.

With a coherent and proclaimable set of biblical values, religion can begin to speak truth to power. There is a curious avoidance of confrontation in the prevalent tendency of contemporary religion to feel it must become expert in every nuance of every problem and then go in full regalia to request from the President or other government leaders that they pay heed to the "expertise" of the community of faith. Rather, they should spend their money establishing unassailable beachheads at the junctions between privilege and need. And from such places they may gather and cry out to power, "See? See what is happening!" Where are the religious leaders of today? They seem so invisible, so sophisticated, so inured to the corporate structures of modernity!

The tragedy of Jonestown is that what seemed such a beachhead was rife with corruptions, permeated at a fundamental point by demonic and evil forces. This does not have to be seen as the inevitable outcome of commitment.

To those suspicious of the Bible as a source of ethical

stimulation, I offer the roster of fallible, human, but saintly persons who have never compromised the freedom of others while crying out the truth of the gospel path.

The late Reverend Jim Robinson was a good example. For years he was pastor of the Church of the Master in Harlem and later head of Crossroads Africa. Jim could go from campus to campus and warmly and firmly press upon young men and women a liberating alternative to an other-directed American lifestyle. I don't know how many Jim convinced to follow the gospel—into the ministry, into various agencies of human service—but I am sure it was in the hundreds. I am speaking of lifetime vocational commitments. Jim did not only preach. He had a structure of service. In the city it was a community center. In the country it was a series of camps. I used to go to these camps for weekends—a relief from college. There was a cluster—perhaps twenty students—who would gather and be introduced by a man named George Twine. George would gather us in a circle. But by the end of an evening, we would all know and value one another, and the next day we would work side by side, and the spirit would be one of fellowship and deep gratitude for a chance to orient life toward commitments that were not stifling or meaningless.

George directed the camp, and I remember that he told us before the kids came in the summer, "Put the children first." It was a simple principle. But what it did was orient community life in such a way that it was focused on a purpose outside itself. I speak of children to such an extent because it is right there in the Gospels and because it is right there in the easy marriages and easy divorces to which religion passively nods its head—and it was right there when George Twine called us to such a conception of community.

Dorothy Day is another example of true religion. Dorothy Day has been the inspiration behind the Catholic Worker movement in America, working with supreme charity and goodwill. She is Roman Catholic. But is she not a Christian saint as well? She has been called an anarchist. But the simple ministry of the Catholic Worker to the hungry and the maimed of society bespeaks a concern with a world of justice and order. She is a beautiful woman who is an inspiration to all who know her.

You the reader know the saints among you. They are everywhere, and many of them are so quiet about their work and so inconspicuous in their devotions (as Jesus suggested we all be) that they could be called invisible bearers of the truth of the Beatitudes. It is the saints as well as scripture that calls us to the values named here. Is there a living saint who will not practice tolerance? Or one who does not reach out to the helpless? Or one who does not somehow speak a word against tyranny and for the rights of human beings to determine their own lives? Proper religion is a seedbed of sainthood; and it becomes that not by being worldly wise but scripturally wise, with a wisdom not of this world. It is by such wisdom alone that the world is transformed.

As mentioned previously, religious institutions may be generally characterized as institutional, intentional, or insular. Specific characterization using no basic values can lead to distortion or even fatuous preoccupation. That is not the purpose of such an effort. The purpose is to arrive at acceptable standards for determining both positive goals and aims and those rare but important instances in which fundamental values have been so perverted that a faith could be called corrupted.

A fitting response to Jonestown by the institutions of religion would be attention to the very values by which we are called to live.

APPENDIXES

The Kinsolving Column

IN A REPORT PUBLISHED on December 15, 1978, *Christianity Today* provided the following item.

"In 1964, Jones applied for ordination within the Christian Church (Disciples of Christ), a 1.3 million-member mainline denomination that is very prominent in the ecumenical movement. John Harms, now retired in Oklahoma, was regional executive minister of the denomination at the time, and he served on the committee that examined Jones. Harms was uneasy about Jones's 'emotion-oriented religious background' and about his lack of seminary training. 'But because he (Jones) seemed to be groping for a more rational approach to religion and because he was an effective leader of the poor and oppressed,' said Harms, 'the committee decided to recommend that People's Temple proceed with his ordination.' Harms, who never heard Jones preach, says he did not favor the decision, believing that Jones needed the discipline of an academic preparation and a good theological foundation."

The first substantial public criticism of People's Temple was a series of articles by the Rev. Lester Kinsolving, published in the *San Francisco Examiner* in 1972. The eight-part series was killed after four installments. There had been extensive picketing of *Examiner* offices by followers of Jones. Kinsolving—who has been criticized by liberal religionists for what they consider to be a jaundiced journalistic approach—also took Jones and People's Temple to task in his syndicated column "Inside Religion." The column was clearly provocative. Kinsolving had his reasons, however, and was reported to have sought the assistance of law-enforcement agencies to investigate the Temple when church authorities resisted his warnings. After Jonestown, Terri Buford, a defector, alleged to a grand jury that Timothy Stoen, the attorney mentioned in the Kinsolving column, had considered plans to have the columnist murdered. Kinsolving deserves a retroactive reward for having spoken out at the time. The full text of the column, which appeared in early 1973, follows.

Pastor 'reincarnated as Jesus' is baffling to disciples of Christ

By LESTER KINSOLVING

Indianapolis, Ind.

National leaders of the 1.4 million-member Christian Church (Disciples of Christ), headquartered here, are either unable or unwilling to do anything about one of their pastors in California who has claimed to be the reincarnation of Jesus Christ.

For when asked about the Rev. Jim Jones, of the People's Temple in Ukiah, 100 miles north of San Francisco, the denomination's president and general minister, Dr. Dale Fiers, told this column:

"There has been no request for any investigation from his region (the Northern California-Nevada Conference); so we are standing behind the church."

But this column has a photostatic copy of a letter written to this regional conference's acting president, Nellie Kratz, asking that the Rev. Mr. Jones' highly questionable healing methods be investigated.

Neither Mrs. Kratz nor the current president, Dr. Karl Irvin, have been willing to take such action regarding such methods as publicly exhibiting, on a pillow, the alleged cancer passed, according to Jones, through the bowels of those he purportedly healed.

The Rev. Mr. Jones has, however, been investigated by the Indiana State Board of Psychology Examiners, and his methods exposed in page one stories in both the Indianapolis Star and the San Francisco Examiner (which paper, 150 of his followers obediently picketed for 18 hours).

The Rev. Mr. Jones, an acquaintance of the late Father Divine of Philadelphia, has done far better in California than in Indiana, which he left in 1965. He was accompanied by several Indianapolis parishioners, who pooled their financial resources and followed him West, because they believed his prediction that the world would end on July 16, 1967.

Now the congregation of People's Temple— with its temple guards who pack .357 Magnums in their holsters (as perhaps the nation's best-armed Disciples of Christ)—accepts the Prophet Jones' (revised) prediction that San Francisco is due at any time now to be bombed into oblivion. But Jesus Reincarnate Jones will give everyone of his flock sufficient advance notice so that they may flee to the safety of one of the caves which pockmark the hills around Ukiah.

Followers of the Prophet Jones now number more than 4,000, and they travel weekly from as far away as Portland and Los Angeles via the Temple's fleet of 11 former Greyhound buses, for services which usually last four or five hours.

The Prophet Jones, 41, is a handsome, glib, charismatic, part-Cherokee Indian, whose flock constitutes an awesome voting bloc in Ukiah (population 10,000). The People's Temple has thus been able to effectively infiltrate such key areas as the school board, the welfare department and law enforcement. (Hence the Ukiah daily newspaper reads as if it were dictated by Prophet Jones, while the radio stations are similarly obedient.)

One of Jones' five assistant

ministers, for example, is Timothy O. Stoen—who also happens to be the assistant district attorney of Mendocino County. Writes assistant D. A. Stoen:

> **"Jim has been the means by which more than 40 persons have literally been brought back from the dead . . . I have seen Jim revive people stiff as a board . . ."**

Five days after receiving this astounding written statement from Stoen, I attended a People's Temple service in which I saw what Jones announced was "the 43rd time that this has happened"—his melodramatic and alleged resuscitation of one of his suddenly stiffened female congregants.

"The registered nurses around her said it was so!" shouted the Prophet Jones. But the only R.N. in sight was his wife.

Yet this amateurish, soap opera salvation apparently had its effect on at least one of the congregation of 1,000 mostly black.

"I know that pastor Jim Jones is God Almighty himself!" screeched an elderly woman, who is among parishioners attracted by the prophet Jones from black churches all over San Francisco.

One of the prophet's former Ukiah colleagues, the Rev. Richard Taylor, who is now a regional officer for the American Baptist Churches of the West, has asked the California attorney general's office to investigate the People's Temple and what he describes as "the atmosphere of terror created in the community by so large and aggressive a group."

But the national hierarchy of the Disciples of Christ apparently has no plans to investigate. This hierarchy includes the Rev. George Beazley, who is currently chairman of COCU, a decaying scheme to merge eight Protestant denominations.

COCU may die even faster when other denominations realize that Dr. Beazley's own denomination is insufficiently organized to handle the Ukiah Messiah.

Two Official
Disclaimers

KINSOLVING'S COLUMN ACHIEVED only part of its purpose. It stirred up the denomination, but not enough to spark an investigation. The Disciples, for one thing, had no tradition of intervening in the autonomous life of member congregations. There was enough consternation over the syndicated column to inspire Dr. A. Dale Fiers, at the time general minister and president of the denomination, to write two letters on February 8, 1973. The first was addressed to denominational leaders; and the second, which Fiers enclosed along with a copy of the Kinsolving column, was a form letter reply to those who were inquiring about the column itself. Fiers called the Kinsolving piece "inaccurate, prejudicial and misleading." The two letters follow.

February 8, 1973

To: Members of the General Board,
   Regional Ministers,
   General Cabinet, and
   Heads of Institutions of Higher Education

Dear Colleagues:

No doubt you have seen or heard reference to the column (copy attached) of Lester Kinsolving concerning the Christian Church

(Disciples of Christ) and the Rev. Jim Jones of People's Temple in Northern California. In order to help answer questions which you may have and to assist you in interpreting this matter to others, I am enclosing a letter which I have written in reply to one inquiry received. It contains the basic information we have to share.

If other questions arise, do not hesitate to write or call me if we can be of help.

Cordially,

A. Dale Fiers
General Minister and President

ADFiers/gd

February 8, 1973

Dear:

Thank you for writing about the article which appeared in your paper under the name of Lester Kinsolving. I fully appreciate the concerns you have raised having to do with the California pastor and the congregation he serves.

The article is inaccurate, prejudicial and misleading. For one thing, the main charge that Rev. Jones claims to be the reincarnation of Jesus Christ has been categorically denied by Jones himself. This was verified for me by Dr. Karl Irwin, the Regional Minister of the Christian Church in Northern California. The charge that national leaders are "either unable or unwilling to do anything . . ." is the writer's own bias and indicates a lack of understanding of Disciples' organization.

It is quite true that the General Office of the Christian Church is not vested with the authority to silence a minister or remove him from his pulpit irrespective of the wishes of the local congregation. When you stop to think about it, would you want it any other way? If so, we could exercise the same authority over your minister and your congregation.

As Disciples of Christ we have cherished a deep belief and long-standing tradition about the freedom of the pulpit and the rights of a local congregation to determine its own internal affairs.

The standing of ministers within the Christian Church regionally and nationally is established under broad policies approved by the General Assembly for the Order of Ministry. The responsibility for granting, reviewing and withdrawing standing is assigned to the regional bodies of the church, in this case the Christian Church in Northern California-Nevada.

We have kept in touch with the regional leaders. They have assured us that they have found no grounds upon which the ministerial standing of this pastor could be justifiably withdrawn.

With best wishes, I remain

Cordially,

A. Dale Fiers
General Minister and President

ADF:11

A Letter from People's Temple

On March 28, People's Temple circulated its own reply to the Kinsolving allegations. It did not actually mention the charges or Kinsolving by name, but its message was clear: Jim Jones was a member in good standing in his denomination. The letterhead was: "Peoples Temple of the Disciples of Christ." The full text follows.

March 28, 1973

Letter to the Pastors,
Disciples of Christ Denomination

Re: Rev. James W. Jones,
     Peoples Temple Christian Church

Dear Disciples Leader:

Our board of trustees at Peoples Temple Christian Church is so very appreciative of the warm Christian fellowship we have constantly enjoyed from pastors such as you who are part of our splendid Christian Church (Disciples of Christ) brotherhood. Because so many of you have been so supportive of our ministry and because God has blessed our work to such an extent that it is becoming increasingly publicized, our board deems it only fair to provide you some background information so as to enable you to answer whatever questions may arise. We have traditionally sought to avoid publicity, even though nearly all that we have received has been very fair and very favorable. So with reluctance we enter a new era and send you the enclosed information, hoping that you will reciprocate by sharing with us your activities as well.

For 22 years Rev. James W. Jones, who is an ordained minister of our Christian Church (Disciples of Christ) brotherhood, has worked to establish a congregation of Christians who would devotedly follow the "simple requirements" of Christ and his apostles, and thereby also be true to the "basic truths" of the Disciples of Christ:

> "Two basic truths were in the minds of the men whose work led to the beginnings of the Disciples of Christ.
> The first was that the church ought to be one without sectarian divisions.
> The second was that the reasons for its divisions were the addition of 'human opinions' to the simple requirements of Christ and his apostles as tests of fitness for admission to the one church, and the usurpation of rule over the church by clergy and ecclesiastical courts unknown in the days of its primitive unity and purity."
> (Garrison and DeGroot: THE DISCIPLES OF CHRIST, A HISTORY, page 11.)

Preaching the literal requirements of Jesus in Matthew to FEED THE HUNGRY, SHELTER STRANGERS, VISIT THE SICK AND IMPRIS-ONED, Rev. Jim Jones has inspired the congregation of Peoples Temple Christian Church to devote themselves to human service in the name of Christ. Describing this "highly regarded" church, the San Francisco Chronicle recently mentioned a number of the charitable activities whereby the church implements Matthew 25:

> ". . . called less formally Peoples Temple, this church is best known and highly regarded for its social works which include housing and feeding senior citizens and medical convalescents, maintaining a home for retarded boys, rehabilitating youthful drug users, and assisting nonmembers as well as members of the faith through college and legal difficulties." San Francisco Chronicle, January 17, 1973.

The ecumenical and social witness of Peoples Temple has led the clergy of other denominations to express their appreciation. Dr. John

Moore, District Superintendent of the Methodist Church for Oakland and the East Bay in California, recently wrote:

"Peoples Temple is a caring community of people of all races and classes. They have the marks of compassion and justice—compassion for the hungry and jobless, lonely and disturbed, and also for the earth and her offspring."

The President of the Ukiah Ministerial Council, Dr. Elmer Schmitt, published a report on churches in the area, stating:

"Progress in meeting the needs of people . . . is perhaps seen most dramatically in the seven-day-a-week program of the Peoples Temple with its team of teachers and lawyers, to mention just a few, who strive in the name of Christ, to serve their fellow men."

The apostolic and "primitive" Christian church quality of the congregational life at Peoples Temple Christian Church is manifest also in plain living and in a sane, subordinated spiritual ministry which takes place in an atmosphere of relative calm and which works in cooperation with medical science. Marceline Jones, wife of the pastor, heads a team of registered nurses who encourage people to consult physicians, often for the first time in their lives. Rev. Jones has often publicly stated that the field of healing should not be left to those who would abuse it or live extravagantly from it, and that although he would personally prefer not to have a healing ministry (so as not to divert attention from becoming Christ-centered, principled Christians), it is a New Testament ministry and a gift from God which he must use as a wise steward.

Our church does not want to be known primarily for a healing ministry even though its results have been medically verified. In fact, one doctor, I. H. Perkins, M.D., stated in a letter:

"To Whom it May Concern:
Reverend Jim Jones . . . has helped numerous individuals obtain cures believed impossible."

In giving credit to God for these cures, Rev. Jones publicly described himself as "only a messenger" of Good.

Rev. James Jones is a graduate of Butler University, has studied deeply into Biblical history and exegesis, spent two years on

128

sabbatical as a foreign missionary establishing programs for orphans abroad, and has, with his wife, Marceline, adopted impoverished children of five ethnic backgrounds.

For many years he had a "tentmaker" ministry, combining the pastoring of a church with being a public school teacher and with being a very successful businessman. He has served with acclaim in many civic posts, including Foreman of the Mendocino County Grand Jury and as Executive Director of the Human Rights Commission for the City of Indianapolis. Last year he was given the Special Merit Award for civic leadership by the San Francisco Sun-Reporter, one of the largest newspapers in circulation in northern California.

My personal enthusiasm and esteem for this God-ordained ministry at Peoples Temple results from it having brought me to Christ from a life of increasing alienation and despair. I was a graduate of the Massachusetts Institute of Technology, a veteran of the Peace Corps, and a graduate student at the University of California (Berkeley) when I first met Rev. Jim Jones. Until then I saw no hope that people of all backgrounds could learn to live together. It was the integrity and character of Jim Jones that convinced me the Christian life could be lived without compromise in this world. It was the close unity of the members that convinced me, a unity that comes from devotion to the teachings of Jesus Christ. I can find no excuse to do other than my best to implement more of Christ's teachings in my life and in my job as a public school teacher.

In conclusion, please let me convey to each of you the very great respect Rev. Jim Jones has for the pastors of the Christian Church throughout the land and its Christ-centered leadership, both general and regional. It is an honor to work for Christ with people such as you. It is additionally an honor to serve in a denomination structurally free to institute ministries under the leading of the Holy Spirit, thus realizing the truth of Romans 12:4–5:

"In our one body we have a number of members, and the members have not all the same function; so, too, for all our numbers, we form one Body in Christ and we are severally members one of another."

If you would like any additional informaton, or if at times we can be of some assistance to you, please do not hesitate to ask.

May God richly bless you.

In Christ,

G. DONALD BECK, Jr.,
Board of Trustees
PEOPLES TEMPLE CHRISTIAN CHURCH
of the Disciples of Christ

Enclosure: Information Sheet

The Reverend
James Jones as
Viewed by Others

THE INFORMATION SHEET accompanying the People's Temple letter indicates that regardless of internal realities, the outward face of the movement in 1973 was explicitly Christian. Partly for this reason what is essentially a public-relations piece warrants inclusion. It is one of many instances in which comments of persons outside the church are used to present the church in a positive light. The piece is entitled "Reverend James W. Jones as Viewed by Others" and is printed in full below.

Reverend James W. Jones is an officially-ordained minister of the 1.4 million member Christian Church (Disciples of Christ) denomination. He has been pastor of his church for 22 years. He is a graduate of Butler University, has studied extensively in Biblical History and exegesis, spent two years on sabbatical as a foreign missionary establishing programs for orphans abroad, and has, with his wife Marceline, adopted impoverished children of five ethnic backgrounds. For many years he had a "tentmaker" ministry, combining the pastoring of a church with being a public school teacher and with being a very successful businessman. During all this time, he has followed the Disciples of Christ tradition of emphasizing the restoration of the "primitive Christian Church" and has worked hard to establish a congregation of Christ-centered, principled Christians who would practice literally the words of Jesus in Matthew 25 to feed the hungry, shelter strangers, visit the sick and imprisoned. The result has been Peoples Temple Christian Church, through which God is doing wondrous things, including the rehabilitation of over 150 young persons from drugs, many of whom are now living in college dormitories provided by the church and are training for careers in medicine and other human service. Invested with the New Testament gift of healing, Rev. Jones exercises this stewardship by carrying on a subordinated, calm, sane spiritual healing ministry known for working closely with medical science. He weekly ministers to three churches in Redwood Valley, Los Angeles, and San Francisco. Rev. Jones' strong belief in the Constitution and Christian citizenship has led to his serving with acclaim in many civic posts, including foreman of the local grand jury and executive director of the human rights commission of a large midwestern city. Last year he was given the Special Merit Award for civic leadership by the San Francisco Sun-Reporter. Rev. Jones and his family live modestly in a cinder-block house with wood trim, exemplifying a deep reverence for all life.

What follows are brief statements about this significant ministry as others see it:

1. *View of Methodist District Superintendent:* "Peoples Temple is a caring community of people of all races and classes. They bear the mark of compassion and justice—compassion for the hungry and jobless, lonely and disturbed, and also for the earth and her offspring."

> . . . Dr. John Moore, Dist. Superintendent of the United Methodist Church for Oakland and the East Bay, Calif. (March 2, 1973) . . .

132

2. *View of Local Clergy:* "(Progress in meeting) the needs of people . . . is perhaps seen most dramatically in the seven day a week program of the People's Temple with its team of teachers and lawyers, to mention just a few, who strive in the name of Christ, to serve their fellow men."

> . . . Dr. Elmer Schmitt, Pres. of the Ukiah Ministerial Association (In Report on Church Progress, published in *Ukiah Daily Journal*, 1971) . . .

3. *A "Christ-Centered" Ministry:* "Pastor Jim Jones has brought me to a deeper relationship with Christ. He is immeasurably Christ-centered and principled in his commitment to serve people. He is usually last in line to get his food and the first to take care of a chore needing to be done. He seems to overflow with love for people and other living things. I saw him speak to a man badly crippled and the man got up and walked away unassisted. Jim, of course, gave the credit to God. I've seen him cup little insects in his hand and tenderly carry them outdoors. Unless I had seen these things first hand, I would never have believed life could be so hopeful. I came to Peoples Temple last summer, and now have the privilege of supervising an innovative cultural-enrichment program for the children. Such meaning my life has!"

> . . . Pat Grunnet, public school teacher and Chapman College graduate (March, 1973)
> . . .

4. *Epitomizes the Giving of Self:* "The Peoples Temple Church, motivated and inspired by their pastor, Jim Jones, epitomizes giving of one's self for human services."

> . . . Marge Boynton (Officer, Republican State Central Commitee, in letter that is dated February 22, 1973) . . .

5. *A "Highly Regarded" Church:* "Called less formally Peoples Temple, this church is best known and highly regarded for its social works which include housing and feeding senior citizens and medical convalescents, maintaining a home for retarded boys, rehabilitating youthful drug users, and assisting non-members as well as members of the faith through college and legal difficulties."

. . . San Francisco Chronicle (Jan 17, 1973) . . .

6. *Its Charitable Activities:* "(There) are the many charitable activities of the People's Temple: a drug rehabilitation program, college grants, convalescent homes, a home for mentally retarded youth, three senior citizens homes, an animal shelter, and emergency legal and medical aid."

. . . Santa Rosa Press Democrat (Jan 18, 1973) . . .

7. *A Growing Church:* "People's Temple ranks as probably the largest Protestant congregation in Northern California, according to various estimates by officials of several Protestant denominations."

. . . Sacramento Bee (October 30, 1972) . . .

8. *The View of a News Bureau Chief:* "While a news bureau chief for the CBS television affiliate in Sacramento, I came to do a feature story on Peoples Temple in November, 1972. I discovered the most dedicated person to the cause of humanity I've ever met. I found Pastor Jim Jones' motives and humanitarian principles to be unquestionably honorable. He is exemplifying the life of Christ by working day and night to relieve suffering and establish true brotherhood, wherever he can. I have become so impressed with the integrity of this humble and selfless man that I recently gave up that position to work full time for this incredible ministry."

. . . Michael J. Prokes, former news bureau

chief for CBS television affiliate in Sacramento, Calif. (March 7, 1973) . . .

9. *A Relevant Church:* "I think Pastor Jim Jones is Godly—and I plan to become a member of the Temple in Los Angeles. I can relate to his teachings. I had not, until a Sunday in December, 1972, been inside of a church for 15 years."

   . . . Editorial Page comment by the Publisher of the Los Angeles Herald-Dispatch (Jan. 18, 1973) . . .

10. *Support for Police:* "(Peoples Temple Christian) Church, which has a congregation in the Fillmore District, has started a fund to aid the families of slain policemen. 'We are utterly horrified by this move to murder police all over this nation,' the Reverend James Jones . . . told the Chronicle yesterday. The Disciples of Christ congregation started off the fund with $150. The money collected will go to the families (of a Berkeley officer and two) officers killed last weekend . . ."

    . . . San Francisco Chronicle (Sept 4, 1970) . . .

11. *Support for a Free Press:* "Twelve newspapers . . . and a newsmagazine and a television station have been awarded grants totalling $4400 by Peoples Temple Christian Church of the Disciples of Christ for use 'in the defense of a free press.' Announcement of the grants was made yesterday in Ukiah, Mendocino County, by the Board of Trustees of the church, which has a statewide membership of more than 7,500. Speaking for the Board, Trustee James R. Pugh said: 'We believe the American way of life is being threatened by the recent jailings of news reporters for refusal to reveal their sources. As a church, we feel a responsibility to defend the free speech clause of the First Amendment, for without it America will

have lost freedom of conscience and the climate will become ripe for totalitarianism."

> ... San Francisco Chronicle (Jan. 17, 1973)
> . . .

12. *Special Citizenship Award:* "It gives me extreme pleasure to announce that you have been selected as recipient of the Sun Reporter 1971 SPECIAL MERIT AWARD . . . Your acquaintances speak glowingly of your numerous social concerns, involving efforts to rehabilitate drug addicts, provision of housing and health care for senior citizens, the development and maintenance of an animal shelter, and your multi-racial adopted family—all of which we believe is encompassed in the Judeo-Christian ethic—that man is his brother's keeper. These are tumultuous times, requiring that each individual be ever mindful of the prophetic words of Edmund Burke, spoken in the 18th century: 'All that is necessary for evil to triumph in the world is for enough good men to do nothing.' "

> ... Carlton B. Goodlet, Ph. D., M. D., Publisher, The San Francisco Sun-Reporter (letter dated April, 1972) . . .

13. *"He was superb":* "The Rev. James Jones will be sorely missed as executive secretary of the Mayor's Commission on Human Rights. He was hired after long search . . . He was superb. He went about his job diplomatically but thoroughly and produced results."

> ... Editorial, The Indianapolis Times (Scripps-Howard), 1965 . . .

14. *A Family Man:* "The man who pastors this flock of 'brothers' is a cross between a fiery archangel, a humble servant of humanity, an erudite wit, a loving family man with all the usual longings for a 'better

life' for his children—and a plain human being who sometimes finds the battle 'heavy going.' "

> ... Kathy Hunter, wife of Editor, of the Ukiah Daily Journal (June 3, 1968) ...

15. *The View of a Seminary Professor:* "James Jones seems to have great qualities. His para-psychological powers are quite extraordinary . . . Obviously this man has some powers (not dissimilar to those of Jesus in the Biblical record) that are beyond those of most of us. His capacity to help sick and decrepit people is also evident . . ."

> ... James Carley, Professor at Christian Theological Seminary (in letter published in the Indianapolis Star, December 22, 1971) ...

16. *The View of a Medical Doctor:* "I have known Reverend Jim Jones for more than one year and have found him to be a dedicated, trustworthy, sincere person who is endowed with an ability and talent possessed by very few. He practices exactly what he preaches, has helped numerous individuals obtain cures believed impossible and all of the while being a considerate, understanding leader of men. It was with pleasure that I attended his services and witnessed his utter, complete involvement. He has saved many from disaster and started them on a meaningful path of constructive well adapted behavior."

> ... I. H. Perkins, M. D. (In a letter "To Whom It May Concern," dated March 2, 1972) ...

17. *Protection of Individual Liberty:* "This church, the Peoples Temple of the Disciples of Christ, has a distinguished pastor, Reverend James W. Jones, and they have never failed to respond to public or private

appeals for assistance in the pursuit and protection of individual liberty and freedom."

.... Publisher, San Francisco Sun-Reporter (In letter to University Dean dated February 5, 1973) ...

The Welcome Tourists

THE FOLLOWING *Washington Post* editorial, dated August 18, 1973, indicates that People's Temple was winning friends and public praise despite the recent first serious criticisms of its internal practices.

The Welcome Tourists

The hands-down winners of anybody's tourists-of-the-year award have got to be the 660 wonderful members of the People's Temple Christian Church of Redwood Valley, Calif.—who bend over backwards to leave every place they visit more attractive than when they arrived. Like thousands of other tourists, they went calling on the U.S. Capitol the other day; but unlike others who tramp through our town spreading litter helter-skelter, this spirited group of travelers fanned out from their 13 buses and spent about an hour cleaning up the grounds.

One 82-year-old woman who was policing the area at the foot of the Capitol explained to reporter Frank Jones that the members take pleasure in sweeping across the country this way. The church, which has black, white and American Indian members, has already won friends in dozens of cities since its tour left Redwood Valley Aug. 8, and still more areas will benefit by the members' stopoffs on their return trip.

139

Wade Rubick's Memorandum

In April 1974, Wade D. Rubick, a member of the Disciples of Christ and the denomination's legal counsel, paid a visit to Redwood Valley to look at People's Temple firsthand. According to the chief information officer of the Disciples, Bob Friedly, Rubick's visit and subsequent writtten observations were "not an investigation. Rubick in reaction to Lester Kinsolving's column took it upon himself to visit the Temple while on the West Coast on other business. Then he offered this report." The report was given to Dr. Kenneth L. Teegarden, Dr. Howard E. Dentler, and Dr. William C. Howland, Jr., and prefaced with this note: "Attached is a memo relative to my brief but interesting visit to People's Temple Christian Church in Redwood, California. After reading it, if you have any comments about my observations, I would appreciate hearing from you." The full memorandum follows.

MEMORANDUM
April 22, 1974

(On April 1 and 2 I visited Peoples Temple Christian Church in Redwood, California. The following are a few observations and opinions of what I observed.)

Eight years and ten months ago Jim Jones and 174

members of an Indianapolis church moved to Redwood, California and started a new church that now involves more than 10,000 persons in Redwood, San Francisco, and Los Angeles, California.

This extended parish is governed by a board of 44 persons (men and women, black and white) who are primarily responsible for financial matters. Major policy and programmatic decisions are determined by a large weekly night business meeting which is generally attended by 500 to 700 persons. Its format is one of participatory democracy.

Peoples Temple Christian Church is heavily oriented toward a Social Gospel ministry. It is integrated with perhaps half of its members from the black race. The church attendance in Redwood is approximately 40 per cent black and this has caused many problems which have led to threats and some acts of violence against Jim Jones and the church. For this reason there is considerable concern for the safety of Jim and at night a watchtower at the rear of the church property and overlooking the parsonage is manned by members of the congregation.

The church building in Redwood is ample testimony of the unusual character of this congregation. The building is one large room that houses a heated swimming pool, the community center and the church. Folding chairs are used for services but when I visited the church it was only a large room with the swimming pool being occupied by a number of younger boys.

I was informed that one of the social concerns of the church is helping to cure drug addicts. To date over 175 persons have been cured from serious drug use. I talked with one of these persons who gave me ample proof of the effectiveness of the church's program in this area of ministry.

A singularly unique program for this congregation is a ranch known as "Happy Acres" where 15 mentally retarded young men and women live. These "guests" are between the ages of 16 and 26. The home is licensed and is staffed by members of the church, two of whom are Jewish. Numerous persons from the church involve themselves in this ministry and their effectiveness is proven by the fact that several of the young men have shown remarkable progress and have been able to work productively in the community.

Happy Acres consists of 40 acres of land, 7,200 grape vines, a large animal shelter, an organic garden, three cottages and a mobile home that is used by two caretakers. Like all of the other homes operated by the church, this one was a model for cleanliness and efficiency.

There are eight (I visited only three) homes which are occupied by older men and women who need help. In one home I talked with three black women who had formerly lived in a Father Divine institution. One was almost 100 years of age.

The homes for the aging were well cared for and staffed by members of the church. They were exceptionally clean and comfortable. A typical home was Hilltop Haven that housed 14 men. Food was prepared in a common kitchen and eaten in a very pleasant dining room. A catfish pond and numerous ducks and geese made the entranceway lively and interesting. This house won a state award several years ago for its excellence.

One of two cottages near the church houses single people who live in a supportive relationship that borders on communal living. In one of these I met a teenage student who before coming to the house was failing in school. However, now he is an honor student with straight A grades. In this same house there also lived a math tutor (an extensive community tutorial program is carried on by the church), a construction worker, an artist, a social worker, a saw mill laborer and some staff from the church.

Twelve Greyhound buses (two have over 1,000,000 miles

on them, I was told) are parked at Redwood. A large garage facility is being constructed to house these buses.

The buses are used to carry members of the church back and forth between the three communities (Redwood, San Francisco and Los Angeles) where the church's members are living. They also take members on vacations at no cost to those who go. And last summer the caravan of buses drove through the South on the way to the nation's capitol. One of the interesting sidelights of this tour was that in Mississippi a white man, after observing the tour members at rest stop, came to one of the tour leaders and in his presence tore up his KKK membership card.

In front of the bus garage is an Operational Center for church activities. It houses a recording studio were Jim Jones tapes sermons and messages that are broadcast from Los Angeles to Canada and in the state of Ohio. The Center also has a printing and publishing business which is now in the process of printing a coloring book for teaching. Nine people were working in the print shop when I visited it late at night.

The Center also has several offices for staff who handle answers to mail that comes in at the rate of 200 to 400 letters a day. Many of these people are volunteers and it was in one of the offices that I met Jean Brown who is a niece of Barton Hunter.

Behind the Peoples Temple Christian Church is a very modest ranch style parsonage where Jim and Marceline Jones and their nine children live. Marceline is a registered nurse and works for the State Welfare Department as a convalescent home supervisor. Eight of the Jones' nine children are adopted. Two are black, one is an Indian and those that I saw or met seemed to be well adjusted normal teenagers.

Behind the Jones' house is another shelter for animals. It houses Mr. Muggs (a chimpanzee who attends all business meetings and rides the buses between Redwood and Los

Angeles), numerous dogs, goats, chickens, etc. This shelter exists for all unwanted animals as part of Jim Jones' concern is a "reverence for life" quite similar to that of Albert Switzer [sic].

In addition to the social programs and concerns mentioned above, the church helps support approximately 150 young people in colleges and universities. It even owns several houses at state schools where some of these students live.

The church also operates two thrift stores, gives endless relief to people in need (at home and overseas), provides medical assistance for those who cannot afford their own, and makes available counseling service to people who need this kind of help. It even provides lawyers and social workers for this purpose and I was told that many of the 80 to 100 calls that Jim Jones receives a day are asking for assistance of this nature. Many times the church has helped get bonds for persons in trouble with the law. It then has assisted in their defense and rehabilitation.

Finally, the church has several long range plans or programs. One of these is to buy land overseas to grow food for relief of starvation in the world. The other is to start a free medical clinic in San Francisco. This latter program is going to necessitate doctors and the church plans on educating several young men for this cause.

Now before ending this report I want to talk about Jim Jones as the church is truly led by this charismatic man. He met me in the church. A macaw was sitting on his shoulders at the time, and for an hour or more he talked about his work, the healing he did, his theology, the church and its people. In many respects I found him to be very liberal in his theology and especially as to the social work that he promotes and helps to administer. He appears very humble, unpretentious, self-sacrificing, completely dedicated and committed to the fulfillment of the Gospel as he understands it.

CONCLUSION

The Peoples Temple Christian Church does not follow in the traditional Disciple mold of what a local church should be like. It is very different and in many respects proved to be an enigma to me. Many questions were left unanswered by my short visit but this was perhaps because I failed to raise them and the answers did not seem to be obvious. However, from my numerous contacts with members and staff of the church, I can say that they are the most committed and dedicated group of people I have known in any church anywhere.

There is no doubt that this congregation would be far less effective in its ministries if it tried to conform to what may be called the "traditional pattern" of Disciples churches. Because of this, I would be one who would discourage the effort. This difference, however, will always cause many well intentioned persons to look with disfavor on this congregation and be suspicious of its successes. But, as long as it is identified by choice with the Disciples of Christ, I believe that it is good to foster this relationship for the mutual good that can be done for both Peoples Temple Christian Church, the regional and national manifestations. Perhaps this church is a very unique demonstration of the wide diversity that can be practiced in a denomination that stands for unity among all persons who walk after the way of our Lord.

—Wade D. Rubick

A Ministry of Human Services

Dᴜʀɪɴɢ ᴛʜᴇ ᴍɪᴅ-1970s, to read the press one would find little criticism in Jones and the People's Temple. The following items give a good sense of the sort of outreach that made the People's Temple prominent and well regarded by the outside world. In each of the pieces the connection with the church is stressed. The first is a laudatory article published in *Insight*, a Seventh-Day Adventist publication, on December 16, 1975. Note that Jones is quoted as condemning Communism.

insight
16 december 75

A Ministry of Human Services

JAMES THURMAN JONES, 43, is known as Pastor Jim Jones to the thousands who are members of his church, the Peoples Temple of the Disciples of Christ denomination. The church has grown from Jones and a few followers meeting in the garage of his home to 10,500 members including congregations in Redwood Valley, San Francisco, and Los Angeles.

Some projects of the Peoples

Temple are care homes for orphans and senior citizens, a forty-acre ranch for retarded children, convalescent centers, college dormitories, and a refuge shelter for animals.

Pastor Jones believes that through such voluntary action programs his church can best help "in combating Communism and other tyrannical systems that threaten a free society."

While Peoples Temple lists its active member rolls at about 10,500 it is estimated that another 10,000 attend services of the three congregations, with many of the latter also involved in the church's wide-ranging projects.

How are the various projects accomplished? Contributions to a church with a congregation ranging from 10,000 to 20,000 are considerable. The church sponsors many money-making events ranging from bake sales to concession stands at baseball games.

Perhaps most important is the contribution of church members, from volunteer labor to the counsel of lawyers, doctors, and numerous ordained ministers who have joined the congregation.

Pastor Jones recently was selected by Religion in American Life as one of the top one hundred most outstanding clergymen in the nation.

Pastor and Mrs. Jones have seven children, six of them adopted from impoverished and different racial and ethnic backgrounds.

Temple Expands Outreach Program

THE SECOND, FROM THE *Ukiah Daily Journal* of January 16, 1976, speaks of Jones's vast humanitarian ministry. The article appeared with a photograph showing Jones receiving the Humanitarian of the Year Award from the *Los Angeles Herald*. He is pictured with fellow church people.

Ukiah Daily Journal, Ukiah, Calif. Friday, January 16, 1976

Vast humanitarian ministry

Temple expands outreach program

Peoples Temple Christian Church, of the nationwide Disciples of Christ denomination of two million members, expanded its extensive outreach program this past year to include a large number of wide-ranging groups, organizations, and causes, all concerned with improving the welfare of the citizenry.

Among those who received financial and other kinds of support from the Temple were the Fresno Bee newsmen arrested for refusing to reveal their confidential sources of information; a medical clinic (Tel-Hi) serving the Bay Area, which otherwise would probably have had to close its doors; the American Cancer Society; the Mendocino County Heart Association and other medical research and testing programs, such as Sickle-Cell Anemia; KQED and other educational broadcasting stations; Big-Brothers of America; anti-hunger groups such as Bread for the World; Indian relief; city schools; hospital development; various church programs operated under Catholic, Protestant, and Jewish sponsorship; the purchase of at least 1,700 concert tickets to benefit the Center for Self-Determination; and many others, the most recent being a donation of $500 to the family of a slain highway patrolman in the Fresno area, for which the Temple was highly praised last week in an article in the San Francisco Chronicle.

The above support was in addition to the Temple's own vast humanitarian ministry, pastored by Rev. Jim Jones of Redwood Valley, which is widely recognized for providing its many thousands of members, and others who are non-members with care homes and convalescent centers; a children's ranch on 40 acres; apartment units for senior citizens; free legal services and health care, including effective drug rehabilitation; bus transportation; college education for young people; food, clothing, and other round-the-clock emergency services; and large refuge shelters for all kinds of animals.

Pastor Jones' ministry is concerned not only with helping to meet the needs of those who are disadvantaged, but also with identifying the causes of those needs so that they might be eradicated from our society. It is because of this consistent and genuine effort that Pastor Jones received the highly coveted award of the Los Angeles Herald as the "Humanitarian of the Year." In a ceremony he was presented with a beautiful painting from internationally known artist Dr. Yvonne Meo, and a trophy.

Thomas Fleming's "Weekly Report" April 21, 1977

THE SUN REPORTER, Thursday, April 21, 1977

Thomas Fleming's Weekly Report

Jim Jones, an independent leader or pastor of a church within the Christian religion, is not well liked by some elements of the Christian religion. We use the term "independent," because Jim Jones is outside the confines of the structured or denominational groups, such as Catholic, Methodist, Baptist, Lutheran, Anglican, or any other that tells its followers that its particular method is the best method by which all those interested in the hereafter may reach the goal of entering into the kingdom of the hereafter.

Jones perhaps looked in his early days, and what he saw caused him the same emotion of disgust that kept Henry L. Mencken all through his lifetime as one of the great agnostics. Jones is the founder of Peoples Temple, a religious organization that follows the precepts of Jesus Christ more diligently than does any other group that professes to follow the teachings of Jesus Christ.

Christ, during his short career among men, preached a philosophy of loving thy brother regardless of color or speech. At least, that is the way in which this writer views Christ and the faith that is named after him—Christianity.

Jones, in his endeavor to make life confortable for all mankind, struck a note of genuine empathy for those persons who had been generally ignored by other prophets or messiahs who claimed direct contact with Christ, when such prophets or messiahs organized their own sects.

Blacks and the other pariah groups mostly were regarded as outcasts, not because they were not also of humankind, but because the other messiahs and prophets were more interested in capturing adherents among the more affluent people of the world who would be in a position to donate generous sums of money. These donations would cram the coffers of the prophets and messiahs who organized so-called Christian sects.

The growth of Peoples Temple has been phenomenal, simply because Jones and his immediate followers have got across to those who comprise the pariah class that there is a group that is genuinely interested in seeing people—all people—become brothers under one common Father—Jehovah.

Jones's success has been a source of trouble for him and for those persons who have become his detractors. Jones first became the target of a so-called holy man, who supplemented his meager income as a preacher by contributing scurrilous writings to a number of newspapers, including the San Francisco Examiner, discussing Jones's methods of defining Christianity for those persons who were looking for some form of spiritual surcease from the vexing problems of everyday living.

But attacks upon the Jones program of the brotherhood of mankind have not decreased one iota. Attacks upon the brotherhood program have been intensified to the same extent that earlier attacks were made against Jesus Christ in his day.

Then there are some members of the boobocrat group here in the United States who find it most unpleasant to behold peoples of different colors and speech worshiping in one and the same temple without any hindrance stemming from those superficial differences. The Jones organization has shown some concern about the vitriolic nature of the criticism that has been directed against it by faceless people who never show themselves. Most of the diatribes have been issued in the form of hate mail, which should be ignored, but one never knows just how far the writers of threatening letters are prepared to go to carry out their written threats.

I cannot, because of space limitations, go into all of the social welfare programs that Peoples Temple has become involved in since its inception, but they are considerable. There has not been one instance where Peoples Temple has ever euchred anyone out of his money so the Temple might conduct its munificent welfare works. These programs are such a vibrant portion of the Christlike religious undertaking that Jim Jones and his followers offer to the polyglot people of this community who call themselves, and who are, American citizens.

Ex-Disciple Calls Cult "Nightmare"

IN AUGUST 1977, there was another Kinsolvinglike explosion. *New West* magazine published a series of articles by Phil Tracy and Malcolm Kilduff alleging numerous instances of misconduct within the People's Temple. At the same time there appeared in the *Indianapolis Star* on Sunday, August 14, an article that could not escape the attention of the Disciples of Christ national staff—located, as it is, in Indianapolis. Under a five-column headline on the front page of the feature section, Carolyn Pickering wrote the story of Rhoda Johnson, a Temple defector. The headline read, "EX-DISCIPLE CALLS CULT 'NIGHTMARE.' " The article refers to a series that had appeared in the *Star* as early as 1972, revealing how Jones lured followers into his fold. This piece and the one following provide clear evidence that the doubts raised by Kinsolving in 1972 and 1973 were valid. I include the piece in its entirety because it offers substantial confirmation in advance of the Jonestown event that all was not well in the People's Temple.

Ex-Disciple Calls Cult 'Nightmare'

By CAROLYN PICKERING

It has been nearly five years since Rhoda Johnson slipped away from the People's Temple at Ukiah, Calif., that is

153

operated by the Rev. James Jones, former Indianapolis Human Relations director.

Rhoda was too frightened to tell her story earlier. She's still apprehensive enough to request that her married name not be published.

"There are those who don't believe what happens in that place is for real. They think I got it out of a book," she declares.

But, Rhoda, now 22, holding down a responsible job and taking advanced training, is ready to relate what she knows about life as a disciple of Jim Jones—the self-styled "prophet of God" who launched his career in Indianapolis and developed enough political clout to be named to the Human Rights Commission post under former Mayor Charles A. Boswell in 1961.

RHODA, NOW FAR from the spartan regimentation the Rev. Jones (just call me Jim) exerted over his flock, the transplanted Hoosier who had convinced his followers he was "the reincarnated Hitler," handpicked to lead a military takeover of the government, now is willing to tell her story to the district attorney at San Francisco.

That office last week opened an investigation into allegations of physical and mental abuse of Temple members.

The inquiry began after an expose in New West Magazine, published at Beverly Hills, Calif., detailed incredible stories given by former Temple disciples, including the wife of the Temple's attorney—himself a former assistant district attorney in the county where the faithful live—Mendocino County.

(The Indianapolis Star, in a series of articles published in 1972, revealed how Jones, appealing to the emotions of the insecure, had lured some 4,000 people to his fold. A few had come forth with frightening stories of life inside the Temple. The Star was inundated with letters and calls from followers of Jones, protesting the series.)

WHILE AFFIDAVITS and depositions today are being taken at San Francisco, where Jones has a temple on Geary Street, the subject of the accusations being made by those once convinced he was "God" has split.

Last week, Jones was reported at his agricultural station at Guyana, South America, a 27,000-acre place he calls the "Promised Land."

Jones sent his resignation as chairman of the San Francisco Housing Authority to the man who appointed him to that politically-influential position—San Francisco Mayor George Moscone—saying he (Jones) no longer had the time to devote to such an endeavor.

For Rhoda, the experience that came dangerously close to "wrecking my whole life," began in late 1970 when she and her older sister, caught up in Jones' preachings, followed him to California.

WHY WOULD A 16-year-old girl want to journey so far away in the first place?

She explains:

"I was like a single ant in the whole world. I was nothing going nowhere. I was bored and unhappy at home. They (Jones) made me feel like I was someone.

"Just the sound of his voice made you feel like you had power. My parents even were caught up by him and they encouraged me to join him," she declares.

(Two years later Mrs. Johnson came to the Star with documentation indicating her daughters were living in an "atmosphere of terror." She had risked her own safety to bring them home. But they refused to discuss their experiences with anyone out of fear of reprisal.)

IT WASN'T UNTIL she learned others in recent weeks had grown disenchanted and were speaking out loud and clear that Rhoda Johnson agreed to talk of her two years as a member of the Jones' flock.

Rhoda believes Jones to be "sick of mind and body." At first, things went serenely enough behind the heavily-guarded Temple grounds at Ukiah, Calif.

"But," Rhoda says, "the pace of living was so strenuous no one could think straight. My daily schedule was to rise at 6 a.m., go to school until noon, work in a Temple-sponsored restaurant in town until evening, spend the evening working in the nursing home until 10 p.m. then go to church until 3 or 4 a.m.

"This went on six days a week. The only night I had off was Monday. I never had more than three hours sleep a night. Jim Jones said that was all that was needed to restore vitality to the body.

"THEN THE BEATINGS began. I was whipped with a belt three lashes each time for such things as calling my parents on the phone or contacting someone on the outside.

"The phones had to be bugged because they always knew what I had said during the outside calls. Jones preached that no one in the outside world was to be contacted . . . that he was 'God' and that's why his hair was 'black as a raven,' like it said in the Bible. Actually, his hair was dyed," she maintains.

The beatings, which Rhoda says were common and were given for a variety of reasons, never were inflicted by Jones himself but by one of his disciples.

Depicting the 46-year-old "Prophet" as a man intent upon military takeover of the government, Rhoda tells of Jones ordering his followers to march for Angela Davis when she, a reported Communist, faced criminal charges several years ago.

"HE TOLD US how we had to vote, for which candidates and he was an admirer of Angela and people like Huey Newton. He liked the Kennedys, too," she says.

She says it was during the long services at night that "Jim would spit on the Bible, stomp on it and demand that we not read it, but to study a book he passed out called Introduction to Socialism."

Rhoda still has the book, with its introduction by Albert Einstein.

Jones preached a holocaust would occur, she says, wherein the people who believed in his teachings would be spared while all others would die.

"One night during a session, we heard a big noise like an air-raid siren," Rhoda says.

"JIM TOLD US only his people could hear that siren, that anyone on the 'outside' couldn't hear it. It was very loud and piercing as though it were a warning to all people everywhere that the world was about to end.

"He kept telling us that if we didn't believe him we should call someone on the outside to learn if they'd heard the siren. Of course, no one did because we knew we'd be whipped, and anyway, we believed him," she asserts.

It was during this kind of service that Jones, according to Rhoda, would assure all that such a holocaust would begin in California, but the real devastation would be in Indiana because "that state is the most prejudiced."

As the months wore on, Rhoda says the mission she once felt would "take me someplace, make me into a worthwhile person," became a horrible nightmare with extrication nearly impossible.

"I WAS GOING crazy," she says. "I had no contact with the outside world. I had no privacy and when I complained, Regina Beam (wife of Jack Beam, one of Jones' closest confidantes) would chastise me saying 'the church has given you everything.' "

One night, Rhoda says, she was made to witness "disciplinary measures" taken against a 17-year-old youth named Dan Pietla.

"Danny now is writing a book about everything and I hope the district attorney will get his story," Rhoda says.

Danny, according to Rhoda, had been intimate with several young girls in the Temple's flock.

On this occasion of "disciplining" Danny, Rhoda says Beam humiliated him by making Danny expose himself, go through some grotesque motions and absorb some comments that "really cut him down."

RHODA SAYS THAT while Danny was subjected to ridicule, Jones himself would brag "about his virility."

When her mother arrived to take Rhoda and her older sister (who still has such a fear she refuses to discuss her experiences) from the Temple's bonds, Rhoda came back to Indiana.

But the scars remained for a long time. Some still are there.

"It's taken five years for me to recover and I still wonder if Jim Jones doesn't have enough power to get out of this investigation," she declares.

"I still have a lot I'm trying to forget but it's hard to put out of your mind the sight of my own nephew being beaten unmercifully by a woman out there just because this baby—he was less than a year old at the time—was crying," says Rhoda.

(That youngster, the son of her sister, now lives with his mother and stepfather in a nearby Indiana city.)

"JIM JONES," says Rhoda, "was trying to create a whole new society . . . one he would rule . . . a new world. He's a sick man, I think, but I did learn one thing from those two years.

"I was made aware of how crooked people are . . . I don't mean stealing as such, but he (Jones) taught us how to use psychology to get people to do things the way he wanted them done. He's a super con man," Rhoda believes.

While Rhoda is willing—even anxious—to do what she can today to save others who may be caught up in the swell of some religious fanatacism, her older sister remains silent, trying to forget the inter-racial marriage she says she was forced into while living at Ukiah.

That marriage was dissolved and the older Johnson girl has since remarried but, says her mother, "she gets hysterical at the mention of religion."

MEANWHILE, ANOTHER Indianapolis mother, Alice Moten, longs for the return of her daughter, soon to be 27 years old.

"Deanna wanted her birth certificate about a year ago so she could get a passport to travel with them . . . I suppose to that place in South America, but I wouldn't send it to her," says Mrs. Moten, a frail woman who says her nerves are "wrecked" over her daughter's allegiance to Jones since 1970.

"I feel she's been hypnotized," says Mrs. Moten, who last spoke to her daughter about three months ago when she called from Las Vegas, Nev., where she claimed to be attending a church meeting.

Mrs. Moten says her family became enamored with the movement years ago when a Jones' disciple, Archie Imes, was pastor of the People's Temple at 975 North Delaware Street.

(It burned to the ground in 1975 after Jones sold the property to the St. Jude Deliverance Center. Fire officials said the blaze was the work of an arsonist but no one ever was charged.)

"WE THOUGHT HE (Imes) was a good Christian," says Mrs. Moten.

"I do so hope and pray someone can do something to get my girl back home," she says, almost prayerfully.

According to New West magazine, Jones' political clout in California has grown from control of Mendocino County down the coast to San Francisco and Los Angeles.

His flock had grown to an estimated 20,000 parishioners, about 80 or 90 percent of them black.

The magazine identified two of Jones' closest friends as Mayor Moscone and Lt. Gov. Mervyn Dynally, a black, both of whom would welcome the control of votes possible from a man considered to be the spiritual leader of thousands of inner-city residents in the state's two largest cities.

People's Temple Correspondence from Guyana

IF CAROLYN PICKERING'S piece was not enough to raise a warning flag, the most prominent national coverage of the allegations against Jones appeared on August 15, 1977, one day later. The report, filling a full page in *Newsweek*, was a serious indictment. It is from this moment that we must date the beginning of the last act. Interestingly, the *Newsweek* piece does not identify Jones or the Temple with the Disciples of Christ, even though the status and designation of the group had not changed. The article represents the most serious published criticism of any local congregation within memory. The charges revealed in it are essentially the same as those later "revealed" after the debacle.

People's Temple put out a report on the progress of the Guyana commune in the summer of 1978. It consisted of an introductory letter to "Dear Friends in the Brotherhood" on a letterhead that affirms the continuing tie with the Disciples of Christ. The text of Matthew 25:35-40 runs down the left side of the page. Letter and report follow.

PEOPLES TEMPLE OF THE DISCIPLES OF CHRIST

Dear Friends in the Brotherhood,

We would like to take this opportunity to share with you and your congregation some small part of the joys and blessings we have received as we have worked to establish our Agricultural and Medical Mission in Guyana, South America. Enclosed is a booklet about the project, ". . . a feeling of freedom . . ." It has been compiled from photographs of life at the Mission, plus commentaries of not only residents, but also some of the many visitors to the project. Truly the photographs bear witness to the true and real happiness that only comes from attempting to follow the example of our faith (I Timothy 4:12).

We would also like to share with you a copy of an article submitted to *The Disciple* by Dr. and Mrs. John Moore who recently returned from visiting their two daughters and grandson at the Mission. Dr. Moore, currently pastor of the First United Methodist Church of Reno, Nevada, has served the church for thirty-four years as campus minister, pastor and district superintendent. Mrs. Moore is a writer who has worked closely with groups concerned with ministry to prisoners and farm workers and their families, and teenagers in need of guidance and counseling.

There is so much yet to be done by all of us to build God's Kingdom on earth. We would be inspired and thankful to know of the works of your congregation in proclaiming the Good News. Thank you for your prayers and support.

Yours in service to Christ,

Mrs. Bonnie Beck

FIRST UNITED METHODIST CHURCH
Reno's First Church—Organized in 1868
John V. Moore, Douglas M. McCoy, Ministers

Dr. and Mrs. John V. Moore have just recently returned from a visit to the Peoples Temple Agricultural and Medical Mission in Guyana, South America, where they visited their two daughters and grandson who are residents there. Dr. Moore, with thirty-four years experience as a pastor, campus minister, and district superintendent of the United Methodist Church, is currently pastor of the First United Methodist Church of Reno, Nevada. Mrs. Moore is a writer who has worked closely with groups concerned with ministry to prisoners and their families, farm-workers, disturbed teenagers and runaways.

The Moores have written the following article to capsulize their impressions of their trip to the remarkable model community established by Rev. Jim Jones and the members of Peoples Temple of the Disciples of Christ.

A VISIT TO
PEOPLES TEMPLE COOPERATIVE AGRICULTURAL PROJECT
JONESTOWN, GUYANA

During the month of May, 1978, we had an amazingly beautiful adventure. We visited Peoples Temple Cooperative Agricultural Project in Guyana, South America.

Because so much adverse publicity has been circulated regarding this heroic cooperative of caring and sharing, we felt it important to share our first-hand experience in a town of 1100 people transplanted from Peoples Temple, Disciples of Christ, in the U.S.A.

Our two daughters, one a nurse and the other a teacher with our three-year-old grandson, had written glowing accounts of their life in this unusual project. We wanted to see for ourselves this new land.

We flew to Georgetown, the capital of Guyana, to the Peoples Temple headquarters, which is a lovely home where we housed with others awaiting a flight to Jonestown, the site of the cooperative. Some of the people we met were planning to retire in Jonestown. One small boy had just had adjustments made on an artificial leg and eagerly awaited the hour-long return flight to the hinterland of Port Kaituma, and then home to the cooperative.

The quaint, attractive government buildings of Georgetown and its friendly Black and East Indian culture in a democratic-socialist country we found most pleasing.

From Georgetown we were flown over a vast ocean of jungle to Port Kaituma where our small plane landed on a tiny air-strip. Members of the Temple met us as our plane arrived and drove us through the exquisite interior region to a turn-off where we observed the sign "Welcome—Peoples Temple Cooperative Agricultural Project."

What a miracle it is! Over eight hundred acres of jungle have been cleared since 1974, most of it within the last year. All along the road we could see rows of cassavas, eddoes, bananas, sugar cane, and citrus groves. Further along the road we saw the "piggery" and the "chickery" and the dairy center worthy of the best in scientific animal husbandry.

What we found at the cooperative was a loving community of people in the true New Testament sense.

Educational facilities and nursery care and equipment are excellent. The school is government accredited, and unusually creative in its approach to the learning process. Teachers are excited by the possibilities for teaching in a setting so different from town and urban schools where they had previously taught.

Medical services under the supervision of a brilliant young doctor, Larry Schacht, are excellent. Larry, a recent graduate of the University of California Medical School in Irvine, is in radio communication with specialists in the United States and South America. His corps of nurses and technicians are well trained, and the scientific equipment is first-class. All retired residents are checked daily. Services are also provided for nearby Amerindians and others needing medical care.

A nutritionist is constantly experimenting with vegetable and fruit products in an effort to discover maximum utilization of food grown in Guyana. The farm is thriving. Meals are a delight and are rich in protein, natural grains and vegetables.

162

Soccer, baseball, a good band, crafts, a library of 8,000 volumes and outstanding teachers provide recreational and cultural opportunities for the youth of Jonestown. Birds and animals have become community pets. The band often plays for Georgetown events. It's tops!

The nurture of children and family life is evident. Jonestown offers a rare opportunity for deep relationships between men and women, young and old who come from diverse racial and cultural backgrounds. Single adults, one-parent families, and nuclear families feel at home in the community.

Jonestown is a mixture of frontier life and contemporary society. The small, neat gardens of the retired residents are in evidence on every pathway. There are opportunities for seniors also to take classes, sew, read, or just to sit. An older woman hoeing her garden brought to mind the words of Micah (4:4)—". . . they shall sit every one under his vine and his fig tree, and none shall make them afraid . . ."

Whereas life is somewhat simple in Jonestown, the latest equipment and techniques are employed, for example in putting up pre-fabricated houses in one day.

Morale is exceedingly high. There is a sense of ownership which is rare in collective societies and not present under private ownership.

We came away from the Peoples Temple Agricultural Project with a feeling for its energy and enthusiasm, its creative, wholesome ways (imagine no television—but weekly movies for all), and an understanding of the fascination and high sense of adventure it holds for its residents.

John and Barbara Moore

Thomas Fleming's "Weekly Report" June 15, 1978

IN A SYNDICATED ARTICLE of September 3, 1977, the *New York Times* entered the journalistic lists. The article, by Wallace Turner, identifies Jones as a "United Church of Christ minister"—a misidentification. The article is interesting primarily for what it adds to the public picture of Jones at the time. It is based on an interview with Marceline Jones and includes the statement that Jones had been chiefly a Marxist who "used religion to try and get some people out of the opiate of religion"; that he had said of the Bible, "Marcie, I've got to destroy this paper idol"; and that in many respects he was a fearful man.

"Jim and I have always felt that if they didn't assassinate him, they'd get him by law. I put my checks in a special fund so Jim could have the best legal counsel." Marceline admits that corporal punishment had been used in the Temple for disciplinary purposes.

In June 1978, there was a counterattack of sorts. Several columns appeared, praising the work of the Guyana project. One of these, Thomas Fleming's "Weekly Report" for June 15, is important for its vision of Jones as one who is being persecuted for his work on behalf of racial equality.

The text of the column which, like many other pieces of favorable journalism, was circulated by People's Temple, follows.

THE SUN REPORTER, Thursday, June 15, 1978

Thomas Fleming's Weekly Report

Despite the fact that Jim Jones has temporarily departed the California scene to begin another career in Guyana, there are former members of Peoples Temple who still would do him physical harm or use the courts to destroy him.

Jones, the sociologist who has used Christianity to aid him in helping those of the human race who need help, was under constant attack by those who have followed a program of hypocrisy in their everyday relations with their fellowmen.

The writer was first attracted to Jones when Peoples Temple had its headquarters in Mendocino County, and when hundreds of persons who had been classified as pariahs by the rich and powerful made pilgrimages to Mendocino County every week, particularly for the Sunday services.

The services conducted by Jones resembled the sermons preached by Jesus Christ during his short stay on Earth. The sermons offered to the masses by Christ so angered the rich and powerful that they conspired to have him put to death.

This writer did not know Jones during his sojourn in the northern part of the state, and he was attracted to him by a series of articles appearing in the San Francisco **Examiner,** by the onetime religion editor, one Robert Kinsolving, who later turned out to be just another Bible thumper from that curious section of the country where the Bible thumpers uphold all of the vicious practices of white supremacy.

Jones brought people of all colors and speech into the fold to worship in peace.

There are many persons who find it difficult to find their

particular niche in life, and such people are in dire need of assistance to find the niche that best suits their needs.

The majority of niche seekers are looking for what can best be described as a utopia, and those who went to Jones were not free of thoughts of searching for a land of milk and honey.

Some of those who did not find their utopia fell away and began to launch bitter attacks upon Jones, which fact was not ignored by a number of publications in the state of California.

These publications immediately began to print lurid stories picturing Jones as a charlatan of the first degree—an individual who claimed super healing powers, an individual who through devious means acquired property and money from some of those who went to him in search of utopia. Jones was also charged with possessing powers of persuasion so great that many of the persons within the organization had abandoned their families to follow Jones.

Of course, law enforcement officials joined the battle against Jones after lurid stories began appearing in public print. Investigations were conducted by law enforcement agencies into Jones's operation, but not a shred of evidence was ever produced that Jones was the four-headed devil he was pictured to be—a devil who violated all laws with consummate aplomb.

Jones is now in Guyana, heading a remarkable project, which reminds one of the pioneers of other days, particularly in the United States, who braved the unknown to carve out homes in uninhabited areas.

Guyana is in South America, and was once a British dependency; it then was called British Guiana. Later on it became a sovereign nation.

The population is largely Black, with a considerable number of former British subjects who emigrated from India in search of a better world during the British reign over that great Asian country.

A Black man is president of the country. It is interesting that all of the Blacks found in the New World were brought to the New World from Africa as chattel slaves. Many of the Blacks brought to Guiana escaped and fled to the interior jungle areas, where they lived with the indigenous Indians as free people. Of course, the people found in the New World by Columbus were called Indians.

Where Jones led his great

trek in Guyana is an area that is a virtual jungle, there before the American pioneers led by Jones disembarked from a boat and hacked out a road through the heavily forested terrain to a designated spot.

More trees and other shrubbery had to be cut and burned before the settlers could erect their first buildings.

Now the cleared area is known as Jonestown, and there are perhaps more than 2,000 people. There are some people with medical skills and other skills that mankind has felt so essential for survival.

Among the new pioneers were several hundred young persons, some of whom left home to go abroad with the permission of their legal guardians.

Some of the onetime legal guardians, some of whom are parents of the young persons in the new settlement in Guyana, have been making rumbles that Jones is a person who should be charged with kidnapping. Furthermore, the allegations are made that, even if Jones did not kidnap any of these persons, he is holding them in Guyana against their wills and that in fact the persons held would be only too happy to rejoin their onetime legal guardians or relatives if they could.

The latest allegations against Jones sound just like so much humbug, just as past allegations sounded before Jones started what seems will be the greatest experiment in his career.

Jonestown is self-supporting. A great variety of crops are produced, which feed this tiny colony of transported North Americans: sufficient crops are raised so that some produce goes to the markets in Georgetown, the capital of Guyana. There is a large hog and poultry development within the commune. Several milk cows were taken from the United States, including one seed bull, which will be the nucleus of large-scale cattle raising in the near future.

The education of the young people did not cease when they went to Guyana, for a number of teachers are among the new pioneers, and a school has been built. The young people are also taught such skills as carpentry, plumbing, repairing motors, and just think of the marvelous recreation facilities in the lush land where they have settled. It is not utopia when one considers Homo sapiens, but it seems that it is the closest thing to it.

Affidavit of Deborah Layton Blakey

IN THE SAME MONTH, June 1978, a radically different version of life in Guyana was presented by Deborah Layton Blakey, who had fled the commune in April. It was the most explicit warning of the possibility of mass suicide. By now the warnings of fearful defectors were being transmitted to the state, not to the Disciples of Christ or other church agencies.

I, DEBORAH LAYTON BLAKEY, declare the following under penalty of perjury:

1. The purpose of this affidavit is to call to the attention of the United States government the existence of a situation which threatens the lives of United States citizens living in Jonestown, Guyana.
2. From August, 1971 until May 13, 1978, I was a member of the People's Temple. For a substantial period of time prior to my departure for Guyana in December, 1977, I held the position of Financial Secretary of the People's Temple.
3. I was 18 years old when I joined the People's Temple. I had grown up in affluent circumstances in the permissive atmosphere of Berkeley, California. By joining the People's Temple, I hoped to help others and in the process to bring structure and self-discipline to my own life.

4. During the years I was a member of the People's Temple, I watched the organization depart with increasing frequency from its professed dedication to social change and participatory democracy. The Rev. Jim Jones gradually assumed a tyrannical hold over the lives of Temple members.

5. Any disagreement with his dictates came to be regarded as "treason". The Rev. Jones labelled any person who left the organization a "traitor" and "fair game". He steadfastly and convincingly maintained that the punishment for defection was death. The fact that severe corporal punishment was frequently administered to Temple members gave the threats a frightening air of reality.

6. The Rev. Jones saw himself as the center of a conspiracy. The identity of the conspirators changed from day to day along with his erratic world vision. He induced the fear in others that, through their contact with him, they had become targets of the conspiracy. He convinced black Temple members that if they did not follow him to Guyana, they would be put into concentration camps and killed. White members were instilled with the belief that their names appeared on a secret list of enemies of the state that was kept by the C.I.A. and that they would be tracked down, tortured, imprisoned, and subsequently killed if they did not flee to Guyana.

7. Frequently, at Temple meetings, Rev. Jones would talk non-stop for hours. At various times, he claimed that he was the reincarnation of either Lenin, Jesus Christ, or one of a variety of other religious or political figures. He claimed that he had divine powers and could heal the sick. He stated that he had extrasensory perception and could tell what everyone was thinking. He said that he had powerful connections the world over, including the Mafia, Idi Amin, and the Soviet government.

8. When I first joined the Temple, Rev. Jones seemed to make clear distinctions between fantasy and reality. I believed that most of the time when he said irrational things, he was aware that they were irrational, but that they served as a tool of his leadership. His theory was that the end justified

the means. At other times, he appeared to be deluded by a paranoid vision of the world. He would not sleep for days at a time and talk compulsively about the conspiracies against him. However, as time went on, he appeared to become genuinely irrational.

9. Rev. Jones insisted that Temple members work long hours and completely give up all semblance of a personal life. Proof of loyalty to Jones was confirmed by actions showing that a member had given up everything, even basic necessities. The most loyal were in the worst physical condition. Dark circles under one's eyes or extreme loss of weight were considered signs of loyalty.

10. The primary emotions I came to experience were exhaustion and fear. I knew that Rev. Jones was in some sense "sick", but that did not make me any less afraid of him.

11. Rev. Jones fled the United States in June, 1977 amidst growing public criticism of the practices of the Temple. He informed members of the Temple that he would be imprisoned for life if he did not leave immediately.

12. Between June, 1977 and December, 1977, when I was ordered to depart for Guyana, I had access to coded radio broadcasts from Rev. Jones in Guyana to the People's Temple headquarters in San Francisco.

13. In September, 1977, an event which Rev. Jones viewed as a major crisis occurred. Through listening to coded radio broadcasts and conversations with other members of the Temple staff, I learned that an attorney for former Temple member Grace Stoen had arrived in Guyana, seeking the return of her son, John Victor Stoen.

14. Rev. Jones has expressed particular bitterness toward Grace Stoen. She had been Chief Counselor, a position of great responsibility within the Temple. Her personal qualities of generosity and compassion made her very popular with the membership. Her departure posed a threat to Rev. Jones' absolute control. Rev. Jones delivered a number of public tirades against her. He said that her kindness was faked and that she was a C.I.A. agent. He swore that he would never return her son to her.

15. I am informed that Rev. Jones believed that he would be

able to stop Timothy Stoen, husband of Grace Stoen and father of John Victor Stoen, from speaking against the Temple as long as the child was being held in Guyana. Timothy Stoen, a former Assistant District Attorney in Mendocino and San Francisco counties, had been one of Rev. Jones' most trusted advisors. It was rumored that Stoen was critical of the use of physical force and other forms of intimidation against Temple members. I am further informed that Rev. Jones believed that a public statement by Timothy Stoen would increase the tarnish on his public image.

16. When the Temple lost track of Timothy Stoen, I was assigned to track him down and offer him a large sum of money in return for his silence. Initially, I was to offer him $5,000. I was authorized to pay him up to $10,000. I was not able to locate him and did not see him again until on or about October 6, 1977. On that date, the Temple received information that he would be joining Grace in a San Francisco Superior Court action to determine the custody of John. I was one of a group of Temple members assigned to meet him outside the court and attempt to intimidate him to prevent him from going inside.

17. The September, 1977 crisis concerning John Stoen reached major proportions. The radio messages from Guyana were frenzied and hysterical. One morning, Terry J. Buford, public relations advisor to Rev. Jones, and myself were instructed to place a telephone call to a high-ranking Guyanese official who was visiting the United States and deliver the following threat: unless the government of Guyana took immediate steps to stall the Guyanese court action regarding John Stoen's custody, the entire population of Jonestown would extinguish itself in a mass suicide by 5:30 P.M. that day. I was later informed that Temple members in Guyana placed similar calls to other Guyanese officials.

18. We later received radio communication to the effect that the court case had been stalled and that the suicide threat was called off.

19. I arrived in Guyana in December, 1977. I spent a week in

171

Georgetown and then, pursuant to orders, traveled to Jonestown.

20. Conditions at Jonestown were even worse than I had feared they would be. The settlement was swarming with armed guards. No one was permitted to leave unless on a special assignment and these assignments were given only to the most trusted. We were allowed to associate with Guyanese people only while on a "mission".

21. The vast majority of the Temple members were required to work in the fields from 7 A.M. to 6 P.M. six days per week and on Sunday from 7 A.M. to 2 P.M. We were allowed one hour for lunch. Most of this hour was spent walking back to lunch and standing in line for our food. Taking any other breaks during the workday was severely frowned upon.

22. The food was woefully inadequate. There was rice for breakfast, rice water soup for lunch, and rice and beans for dinner. On Sunday, we each received an egg and a cookie. Two or three times a week we had vegetables. Some very weak and elderly members received one egg per day. However, the food did improve markedly on the few occasions when there were outside visitors.

23. In contrast, Rev. Jones, claiming problems with his blood sugar, dined separately and ate meat regularly. He had his own refrigerator which was stocked with food. The two women with whom he resided, Maria Katsaris and Carolyn Layton, and the two small boys who lived with him, Kimo Prokes and John Stoen, dined with the membership. However, they were in much better physical shape than everyone else since they were also allowed to eat the food in Rev. Jones' refrigerator.

24. In February, 1978, conditions had become so bad that half of Jonestown was ill with severe diarrhea and high fevers. I was seriously ill for two weeks. Like most of the other sick people, I was not given any nourishing foods to help recover. I was given water and a tea drink until I was well enough to return to the basic rice and beans diet.

25. As the former financial secretary, I was aware that the Temple received over $65,000 in Social Security checks per month. It made me angry to see that only a fraction of the

income of the senior citizens in the care of the Temple was being used for their benefit. Some of the money was being used to build a settlement that would earn Rev. Jones the place in history with which he was so obsessed. The balance was being held in "reserve". Although I felt terrible about what was happening, I was afraid to say anything because I knew that anyone with a differing opinion gained the wrath of Jones and other members.

26. Rev. Jones' thoughts were made known to the population of Jonestown by means of broadcasts over the loudspeaker system. He broadcast an average of six hours per day. When the Reverend was particularly agitated, he would broadcast for hours on end. He would talk on and on while we worked in the fields or tried to sleep. In addition to the daily broadcasts, there were marathon meetings six nights per week.

27. The tenor of the broadcasts revealed that Rev. Jones' paranoia had reached an all-time high. He was irate at the light in which he had been portrayed by the media. He felt that as a consequence of having been ridiculed and maligned, he would be denied a place in history. His obsession with his place in history was maniacal. When pondering the loss of what he considered his rightful place in history, he would grow despondent and say that all was lost.

28. Visitors were infrequently permitted access to Jonestown. The entire community was required to put on a performance when a visitor arrived. Before the visitor arrived, Rev. Jones would instruct us on the image we were to project. The workday would be shortened. The food would be better. Sometimes there would be music and dancing. Aside from these performances, there was little joy or hope in any of our lives. An air of despondency prevailed.

29. There was constant talk of death. In the early days of the People's Temple, general rhetoric about dying for principles was sometimes heard. In Jonestown, the concept of mass suicide for socialism arose. Because our lives were so wretched anyway and because we were so afraid to contradict Rev. Jones, the concept was not challenged.

30. An event which transpired shortly after I reached Jonestown convinced me that Rev. Jones had sufficient control over the minds of the residents that it would be possible for him to effect a mass suicide.

31. At least once a week, Rev. Jones would declare a "white night", or state of emergency. The entire population of Jonestown would be awakened by blaring sirens. Designated persons, approximately fifty in number, would arm themselves with rifles, move from cabin to cabin, and make certain that all members were responding. A mass meeting would ensue. Frequently during these crises, we would be told that the jungle was swarming with mercenaries and that death could be expected at any minute.

32. During one "white night", we were informed that our situation had become hopeless and that the only course of action open to us was a mass suicide for the glory of socialism. We were told that we would be tortured by mercenaries if we were taken alive. Everyone, including the children, was told to line up. As we passed through the line, we were given a small glass of red liquid to drink. We were told that the liquid contained poison and that we would die within 45 minutes. We all did as we were told. When the time came when we should have dropped dead, Rev. Jones explained that the poison was not real and that we had just been through a loyalty test. He warned us that the time was not far off when it would become necessary for us to die by our own hands.

33. Life at Jonestown was so miserable and the physical pain of exhaustion was so great that this event was not traumatic for me. I had become indifferent as to whether I lived or died.

34. During another "white night", I watched Carolyn Layton, my former sister-in-law, give sleeping pills to two young children in her care, John Victor Stoen and Kimo Prokes, her own son. Carolyn said to me that Rev. Jones had told her that everyone was going to have to die that night. She said that she would probably have to shoot John and Kimo and that it would be easier for them if she did it while they were asleep.

35. In April, 1978, I was reassigned to Georgetown. I became determined to escape or die trying. I surreptitiously contacted my sister, who wired me a plane ticket. After I received the ticket, I sought the assistance of the United States Embassy in arranging to leave Guyana. Rev. Jones had instructed us that he had a spy working in the United States Embassy and that he would know if anyone went to the embassy for help. For this reason, I was very fearful.

36. I am most grateful to the United States government and Richard McCoy and Daniel Weber; in particular, for the assistance they gave me. However, the efforts made to investigate conditions in Jonestown are inadequate for the following reasons. The infrequent visits are always announced and arranged. Acting in fear for their lives, Temple members respond as they are told. The members appear to speak freely to American representatives, but in fact they are drilled thoroughly prior to each visit on what questions to expect and how to respond. Members are afraid of retaliation if they speak their true feelings in public.

37. On behalf of the population of Jonestown, I urge that the United States Government take adequate steps to safeguard their rights. I believe that their lives are in danger.

I declare under penalty of perjury that the foregoing is true and correct, except as to those matters stated on information and belief and as to those I believe them to be true.

Executed this 15 day of June, 1978 at San Francisco, California.

DEBORAH LAYTON BLAKEY

Official Disciples of Christ Reaction to Jonestown

ON NOVEMBER 21, 1978, three days after the mass suicide, Dr. Kenneth Teegarden, who succeeded Dr. Fiers as head of the Disciples denomination, issued a statement to the press and to thirty-five denominational regional ministers and to some twenty-five Disciples pastors who had made inquiries. The statement was included in the following press release, issued by the Disciples on November 22. Also included is a letter written by Dr. Teegarden on November 22.

78a-188
November 22, 1978   for immediate release

Contact: Lillian Moir, director of news service

INDIANAPOLIS, Ind.—The Guyana mass murder-suicide tragedy involving a minister and congregation related to the Christian Church (Disciples of Christ) may force the Disciples to consider a procedure for disavowing a congregation.

Dr. Kenneth L. Teegarden, general minister and president of the church, has indicated he will ask the church's deliberative bodies to weigh the question.

The Disciples' Design for the Christian Church, the document under which the church operates, describes procedures only for congregations withdrawing at their own initiative.

The People's Temple of Redwood Valley, Calif., has been listed as a congregation of the Disciples of Christ since 1960, when the congregation was located in Indianapolis.

Pastor Jim Jones had been ordained in Indianapolis in 1964. His ministerial standing was under review by the Northern California-Nevada region when the bizarre killings took place at the Guyana agricultural colony founded by Jones.

Following the killing of a congressman and some newsmen who were in Guyana to investigate reports of mistreatment of People's Temple members there, Jones, his wife and more than 900 members of the church died, apparently in a suicide pact.

Disciples leaders in Indianapolis quickly assured church members in response to a flood of telephone questions:

—People's Temple received no outreach money of the denomination and its Guyana colony was totally unrelated to the overseas ministries of the Disciples.

—People's Temple was totally unrelated to the historic home mission center, All People's, in Los Angeles, with the similarity of names being only coincidence.

—The ministerial standing of Pastor Jim Jones had been under review by the Northern California-Nevada region of the church but had not been completed because of the necessity of confronting Jones and he had remained out of the country.

—The Disciples of Christ have no procedure for judging a congregation unfit and removing it from the denominational year book.

It was the latter that brought Dr. Teegarden to the decision to have the representative bodies of the church consider whether such a procedure is warranted.

It would be a major step for the Christian Church because of strong feelings against judgment of one group of Christians by others, part of a denominational heritage of freedom of opinion and practice.

Dr. Teegarden issued the following statement:

"The horrible sequence of events in Guyana is all the more shocking to us in view of the involvement of a minister and California congregation related to the Christian Church (Disciples of Christ). We are deeply anguished by this mammoth tragedy and express sympathy to the families in the United States that lost loved ones. We also express a sincere pastoral concern for the innocent persons of People's Temple in California who may have been victimized in their religious zeal.

"The congregational autonomy of a denomination such as ours, and the resultant tenuous relationships with many local churches, of which we have 4,416, left with us a bare knowledge that People's Temple of Redwood Valley, Calif., had a Guyana colony and no appreciation of a fanaticism that could have led to the human destruction that took place.

"Under our church polity, it is neither possible, nor has it been desirable, to conduct investigations of the activities or ministries of local congregations. We have stood firmly for a variety of styles and approaches to Christian mission and ministry. However, because of this awesome tragedy, we will initiate, at the earliest possible moment, a proposal to determine whether this denomination, which has prided itself on an openness to congregations as well as individuals, wants to develop a procedure, which it does not now have, for removing congregations from fellowship."

When James W. Jones affiliated with the Disciples and during his ministry in Indianapolis there was no forewarning of what was to come. His early ministry was considered something of a model for inner city work, with strong interracial aspects and community service to the poor.

He was graduated from Butler University in 1961, an institution founded by and still related to the Disciples, but he attended no Disciples seminary. He was ordained in June of 1964 by Broadway Christian Center, a Disciples social service project in Indianapolis.

Though People's Temple did not receive any denominational money, it did contribute to the church's outreach, though not nearly as much as some press reports.

The most recent Year Book and Directory of the Christian Church showed $900 given to the Disciples by People's Temple in 1977. That was a figure from Church Finance Council records.

The last report to the Year Book and Directory of the church filed by People's Temple was received July 25, 1977. It listed $100,000 given to interdenominational causes and community action projects in the most recent year and claimed credit for them, but did not specify the causes served.

November 22, 1978

Dear Friends:

The shocking events at Jonestown in Guyana have brought many questions and concerns from Disciples of Christ all over North America. I am taking the unusual step of sending you a copy of a news release prepared for publication by our office of communication as one additional means of fully informing you on the matter.

I would say in addition to what is said in the news release that we should not attempt to minimize our relationship to both the minister and the congregation involved in this horror but should take the opportunity to explain in public who we really are and what we stand for in terms of diversity and freedom within unity.

One Pennsylvania newspaper editor, after a visit from a local pastor and the regional minister who went non-complaining and non-defensively with the Disciples' story, suggested that such press visits might be a wise move for pastors in other communities. I offer that as counsel from an outside professional.

We need your prayers for our church and for the whole world as we deal increasingly with cults and sects, Messiah complexes, and a penchant for violence, which, as we have seen, can touch very close to home.

Sincerely,

Kenneth L. Teegarden
General minister and president
KLT:mh

George Cornell's Report

ON NOVEMBER 29, 1978 the Disciples' position was interpreted by George Cornell of the Associated Press in the following column.

As an old Roman adage puts it, "The worst is a corruption of the best." That might be partly what produced the horror in Guyana of the People's Temple colony whose California base ostensibly was a Christian church.

Somehow its heralded "light" had been inverted into deadly darkness.

"How it could happen in any kind of church is almost beyond comprehension," says the Rev. Kenneth L. Teegarden of Indianapolis, general minister and president of the Christian Church (Disciples of Christ), the denomination with which People's Temple was affiliated.

"Somewhere along the way, something happened to turn a group that had been outgoing and concerned with the needs of people into an oppressive, cultic type of faith bound to a leader who claimed he himself was the truth and who arbitrarily laid down the path to follow."

That authoritarian control was the total opposite of the "free church" tradition upheld by the denomination with which the Temple was affiliated.

The denomination, a mainline, Protestant body born on American soil of an early 19th century movement for Christian unity, always has emphasized the autonomy both of its 4,416 congregations and their 1.3 million members, free of any external controls.

"It was a weird deviation," Teegarden said of the submissive thralldom into which the Temple colony had been twisted by the domineering leader, the Rev. Jim Jones, to the point of mass suicide at his bidding.

The grisly and bewildering affair particularly shocked denominational leaders, who also recognized that anti-religious forces would use the bizarre aberration to blame it on effects of church teaching and Christianity itself.

"There'll be all kinds of interpretations," Teegarden said in an interview. "But it's hardly valid to evaluate Christianity on the basis of a single instance that was an utter contradiction of the gospel message."

To do that, he noted, would be about as illogical as condemning the human race on the basis of individual deviant or criminal behavior.

He said that under his denomination's "free church" system, in which congregations choose their own ministers and which gives room for varied styles and approaches to faith, denominational offi-cials have only a "tenuous relationship" with congregational practices.

This "left us only with a bare knowledge" of the Guyanese colony, he said, and "with no awareness of the fanatacism" that led to victimizing of Jones' followers and the "awesome tragedy" of their suicides.

"We've prided ourselves on our openness and non-judgmental stance toward congregations and individuals," he said. "But in light of this horrible thing, the question now is whether we want in our free church tradition some process for removing a congregation from fellowship."

He said a proposal would be made to determine whether to establish such a procedure. The denomination now lacks any provisions for it.

Nevertheless, more than a year ago, the denomination's Northern California-Nevada Region, with offices in Oakland, Calif., had set up an inquiry committee to examine reports of mistreating of members of People's Temple and mishandling of their property.

Doris McCullough, regional vice-president, said the committee had held numerous sessions but had been unable to complete its recommendations because it felt a duty to first confront Jones with the accusations, and it had been unable to reach him.

The Temple affiliated with the denomination in 1960, and Jones was ordained in it. However, his wife said in a 1977 interview with the New York Times that her husband had not entered the ministry because of religious faith, but because he saw religion as a means of achieving a Marxist social system.

Devotion to Marxist Communism, rather than to Christianity, along with fear and hostility toward society, characterized the notes of followers to Jones, whom they called "Dad," found after their mass poisoning at his command.

The group had "become a perversion of my understanding of Christianity," Mrs. McCullough said. "Anytime a person sets himself up as the way and the answer, ruling out individual reason, it's apt to become destructive. We were given minds as well as souls, with a responsibility to use those minds."

Sermon of John V. Moore

FOLLOWING THE TRAGEDY, the Rev. John Moore, who had written glowingly of Guyana, preached the following sermon. It appeared with an introduction in the December 1978 *United Methodist Reporter*. As will be obvious, this was a personal tragedy beyond all ordinary bounds.

'How did your children become involved in People's Temple?'

The shocking tragedy in Jonestown, Guyana directly touched the lives of the Rev. and Mrs. John V. Moore of Reno, Nevada. Two of their daughters and a grandson were members of the People's Temple residing in Jonestown and are presumed to have died there. Mr. Moore delivered the sermon which follows at the First UMC in Reno, where he is pastor, on the Sunday following news of the

Mass Murder-Suicide in Guyana, noting: "I am preaching this morning because we alone can make our unique witness, and today is the day to make it."

By John V. Moore

During these past days we have been asked frequently: "How did your children become involved in People's Temple?"

There is no simple answer.

We are given our genetic ancestry. We are given our families. We are all on our personal journeys. All of these, along with the history of the race, converge upon the present wherein we make choices. Through all of this, providence is working silently and unceasingly to bring creation to wholeness.

I will talk only of our children's personal histories. The only way you can understand our children is to know something of our family. In our family you can see the relationship between the events of the sixties and this tragedy, just as there is a relationship between the self-immolation of some Americans during those years and the mass murder-suicide of last week.

Our children learned that mothering is caring for more than kin. Dad talked about it from the pulpit. Mother acted it out. More than 15 teenagers and young adults shared our home with our children. Some were normal, but others had problems. One did not say a word for three months. At least two others were suicidal. One young man had come from a home where his father had refused to speak to him for more than a year. From child-

hood our girls saw their mother respond to people in need—from unwed mothers to psychotic adults and the poor.

Carolyn loved to play, but as president of the MYF she pushed the group to deal with serious issues. She had a world vision. She traveled to Mexico with her high school Spanish class. Four years later she spent a year studying in France. At college she majored in international relations. As a member of People's Temple, she stood with the poor as they prepared for and stood in court. She expressed her caring both in one-to-one relationships and as a political activist.

From 1963 until 1972 when Annie left home, Annie and Becky walked with us in civil rights and anti-Vietnam War marches. We were together in supporting the farm worker's struggle to organize. They stood in silent peace vigils. In high school they bore witness to peace with justice in our world. Their youth group provided a camping experience for foster children. When Annie was 16, she worked as a volunteer in Children's Hospital in Washington, D.C. She worked directly with the children, playing with them, playing her guitar and singing. The chil-

184

dren loved her. She decided that she wanted to work in a burn unit, which she did at San Francisco General Hospital before going to Guyana.

Our children took seriously what we believed about commitment, caring about a better, more humane and just society. They saw in People's Temple the same kind of caring people and commitment to social justice that they had lived with. They have paid our dues for our commitments and involvement.

What went wrong?

The second question we have been asked is: "What went wrong?" What happened to turn the dream into a nightmare? I shall mention two things that were wrong from the beginning. These are idolatry and paranoia. I speak first of idolatry.

The adulation and worship Jim Jones' followers gave him was idolatrous. We expressed our concern from the first. The First Commandment is the first of two texts for my sermon. "Thou shalt have no other gods before me." Our children and members of People's Temple placed in Jim Jones the trust, and gave to him the loyalty, that we were created to give God alone.

It's not that they were so different from other mortals, for idolatry has always been easy and popular. The more common forms of idolatry are to be seen when people give unto the state or church or institution their ultimate devotion. The First Commandment says "No!" and warns of disastrous consequences for disobedience. The truth is that the Source of our lives, the One in whom we trust and unto whom we commit our lives, is the Unseen and Eternal One.

To believe the First Commandment, on the other hand, affirms that every ideal and principle, every leader and institution, all morals and values, all means and ends, are subordinate to God. This means that they are all subject to criticism. There was no place for this criticism in People's Temple.

The second thing that was wrong was paranoia. This was present through the years that we knew People's Temple. There is a thin line separating sensitivity to realities from fantasies of persecution. Jim Jones was as sensitive to social injustice as anyone I have ever known. On the other hand, he saw conspiracies in the opposition. I remember painfully the conversation around the table the last night of our visit to Jonestown. Jim and other leaders were there. The air was heavy with fears of conspiracy. They fed each other's fears. There was no voice to question the reality of those fears.

As their fears increased, they increased their control over the members. Finally their fears overwhelmed them.

Our relation to that tragedy

The death of hundreds and the pain and suffering of hundreds of others is tragedy. The tragedy will be compounded if we fail to discern our relation to that tragedy. Those deaths and all that led up to them are infinitely important to us. To see Jonestown as an isolated event unrelated to our society portends greater tragedy.

Jonestown people were human beings. Except for your caring relationships with us, Jonestown would be names, "cultists," "fanatics," "kooks." Our children are real to you, because you know and love us. Barbara and I could describe for you many of the dead. You would think that we were describing people whom you know, members of our church. If you can feel this, you can begin to relate to the tragedy.

If my judgment is true that idolatry destroyed People's Temple, it is equally true that few movements in our time have been more expressive of Jesus' parable of the Last Judgment of feeding the hungry, caring for the sick, giving shelter to the homeless and visiting those in prison than People's Temple. A friend said to me Friday, "They found people no one else ever cared about." That's true. They cared for the least and last of the human family.

The forces of life and death— building and destroying—were present in People's Temple. Death reigned when there was no one free enough, nor strong enough, nor filled with rage enough, to run and throw his body against a vat of cyanide spilling it on the ground. Are there people free enough and strong enough who will throw themselves against the vats of nuclear stockpiles for the sake of the world? Without such people, hundreds of millions of human beings will consume the nuclear cyanide, and it will be murder. Our acquiescence in our own death will make it suicide.

The forces of death are powerful in our society. The arms race, government distant from the governed, inflation, cyber-nation-unemployment are signs of death. Nowhere is death more visible than in the decay of our cities. There is no survival for cities apart from the creation and sustenance of communities within. Cities governed by law, but without a network of communities which support members and hold them accountable, these cities will crumble, and will bring down nations.

This is what made the Jones-town experiment so important for us. It was an effort to build this kind of common life. Its failure is our loss as we strug-gle against the forces of death in our cities.

God is making all things new

I have talked of history and our personal histories, of our journeys and our choices. Providence is God's working with and through all of these. God has dealt with tragedy before, and God is dealing with tragedy now. We are witnesses to the resurrection, for even now God is raising us from death. God whom we worship is making all things new.

Our Lord identified with the least of humans. Christ is pres-ent in the hungry and lonely, the sick and imprisoned. Christ, the love and power of God, is with us now. In Christ we are dying and are being raised to new life.

My last words are of our children. We have shared the same vision, the vision of jus-tice rolling down like a mighty stream, and swords forged into plows. We have shared the same hope. We have shared the same commitment. Caro-lyn and Annie and Kimo served on a different field. We have wished that they had chosen ours, but they didn't. And they have fallen. We will carry on in the same struggle until we fall upon our fields.

No passage of scripture speaks to me so forcefully as Paul's words from Romans: "Nothing, absolutely nothing can separate us from the love of God we have known in Christ Jesus our Lord." This week I have learned in a new way the meaning of these words of Paul: " . . . love never ends."

Now may the Word which calls forth shoots from dead stumps, a people from dry bones, sons and daughters from the stones at our feet, babies from barren wombs, and life from the tomb, call you forth into the new creation.

Reaction of
Dr. William Bright

IN GENERAL, INSTITUTIONAL religious response to Jonestown seemed to concern itself with severing any possible relationship between People's Temple and legitimate institutions of faith. The following Religious News Service report addresses the dominant concern.

RELIGIOUS NEWS SERVICE, WEDNESDAY, DECEMBER 13, 1978

DON'T LINK CULTS, CHRISTIAN AGENCIES, CAMPUS CRUSADE LEADER TELLS MEDIA

By Religious News Service (12-13-78)

SAN BERNARDINO, Calif. (RNS)—Dr. William R. Bright, president and founder of Campus Crusade for Christ International, has warned the news media against confusing "legitimate Christian organizations" with cults like the People's Temple.

Describing the deaths of some 900 members of the cult as "a tragedy that has jolted and appalled the world," Dr. Bright added, "Unfortunately, there seems bound to be some spillover from that tragic event onto legitimate Christian organizations, but it is urgent that the news media do all in their power to avoid damaging valid ministries which have nothing of substance in common with the Jones group or cults in general."

The Campus Crusade leader advised journalists to examine

various groups to determine whether they exemplify "dedication to the deity and lordship of Jesus Christ, to the Bible as the revealed word of God, and to a spirit of Christian love."

Dr. Bright noted that "not all groups are what they seem to be, and it is proper that especially pastors and Christian laymen be interested in the doctrines and practices of organizations which represent themselves as coming in Christ's name. There could be no more striking example of this problem than the People's Temple situation."

According to the Campus Crusade leader, if "God alone is honored as the object of worship, the Holy Scriptures are used as the guide to behavior, and Christian love is practiced as the basis of relationships, an organization can in no fair way be considered a 'cult.' "

Campus Crusade for Christ is an interdenominational ministry of Christian evangelism and discipleship with some 6,500 full-time staff members in 97 countries and protectorates around the world. It ministers to students, prisoners, persons in the ministry, and pastors.

Temple Agricultural Report

THE ROLE OF PROPAGANDA before, during, and after Jonestown would make a fascinating study in itself. Such a study would need to dwell not only on the obvious means by which institutions use any positive input they can get to maximize their public image—that is an accepted and in some respects useful activity. It would need to dwell more on the effect of such publicity in creating pictures of Jones and his activities; it might also concern the role of negative publicity. In general, the revelations about Jones that appeared after Jonestown had also appeared before, yet there seemed a need after the event to create an ascendingly negative portrait. Other questions bearing on propaganda are, What prevented the transcripts of the tape recording of the actual proceeding from being released as soon as it was available? What was the degree of reliance on the stories of particular defectors for a true picture of life within the Temple? How reliable were those accounts? What are the pressures on journalists to produce a "good" picture of religious institutions? What is the role of the religious press in examining cults, institutional self-aggrandizement, misuse of funds, etc?

The following from the Guyana commune is what may indeed have been, for some, a description of the basic reality. It is a progress report of the People's Temple

Agricultural Project (as Jonestown was generally known within People's Temple circles). Portions of the text appear as follows.

PEOPLES TEMPLE
AGRICULTURAL PROJECT
Progress Report—Summer 1977

Introduction

The Peoples Temple Agricultural Project was initiated by Rev. Jim Jones in December of 1973. He conceived of the project in order to assist the Guyanese Government in a small measure, to feed, clothe, and house its people, and at the same time to further the human service goals that have characterized Peoples Temple for many years. The government allotted 3,824 acres in the North West District near Port Kaituma to the project. In October of 1974 the first ground was cleared—a 30 acre plot that fell by hand and by machine, near the spot where 11 were housed in a bark cottage.

Hundreds of acres are now cleared and under cultivation, and housing for nearly a thousand people has been constructed, the last of the housing being constructed with our own pre-fabricated siding. The sawmill operates 24 hours a day. Other innovations include a cassava processor, a planter, and a hammermill temporarily in operation until the government mill in Port Kaituma starts into operation. We've acquired 9 vehicles, including 2 Caterpillar tractors, a dump truck, a crane, 3 large farm tractors, a small garden tractor and a pickup truck.

The agricultural experimenters are learning by trial and error how to produce nutritious crops that, in some cases, have never been tried on jungle soil, and the settlers are learning the art of cooperative living in a wholesome, satisfying and challenging environment. Realistically, we can now expect that the farm will become self-sufficient within three to five years. In the meantime, Peoples Temple members in the U. S. A. are contributing to keep the settlement going through these initial years. We are cooperating fully with the government's plan to buy local products, and we have begun manufacturing our own clothing in accordance with this plan.

The agricultural results are especially heartening to those who have put their "labor of love" into the project during these first few years. Other programs now under way are equally exciting. An educational program provides a balanced curriculum for 135 children, ages 3 to 18. Some youngsters who were said to have learning disabilities in their former setting are quick and willing learners in this cooperative environment. Many of the most extensive projects are supervised by young people whose talents never had the opportunity to develop before. Seniors who were wanting for something to do are now engaged in satisfying programs that enhance their sense of accomplishment in their later years. The cooperative kitchen, which serves three meals a day, produces nutritious and delicious recipes using homegrown foods. It also provides two snacks a day for several hundred people.

Guyana's healthy and pleasant climate (the temperature stays between 65° and 85°F. and the trade winds have a tempering effect), the wholesome atmosphere, and the constructive life style offered by this pioneering project have impressed us deeply with the role Guyana has to play in the future of the Caribbean and the rest of the developing third world. We are deeply pleased to be able to participate. The expectations of Rev. Jones and this government are stimulating our project to be a success of many dimensions.

Guyana: a brief note

Guyana, formerly the colony of British Guiana, achieved its independence in 1966. Though it is part of the South American mainland, Guyana has Caribbean cultural roots. The English-speaking population of nearly one million is mostly black and East Indian, in addition to native Amerindians, along with Chinese and Portuguese inhabitants. Free from an oppressive heritage of slavery and colonialism, Guyana is undertaking to manage, develop, and control its own abundant resources. The nation is especially rich in bauxite. Though the majority of the population lives on the coastal plain, efforts have been underway to develop Guyana's rich interior. Peoples Temple's agricultural mission is part of that effort. It is the goal of the Guyanese government to insure that all of its population is adequately fed, clothed, and housed in the very near future. Though a young and relatively small nation, Guyana has taken a leadership role in the community of non-aligned nations pursuing a socialistic course.

Agriculture

MAJOR CROPS

Major crops include the bitter and sweet cassava, sweet potatoes, eddoes, papaya and dasheen. Here are brief descriptions of our experiences with some of these:

Eddoes: This has been one of our major crops from the start. We eat both the tubers and the greens. We had to clear the original planting site, which was thick jungle. The felled trees were left for a burn, and the first eddoes were planted between the burnt logs. We are now planting in well-prepared beds, 900 feet long, 2 feet apart, with good drainage ditches. Shells, TSP, and potash are applied for fertilizer. We are weeding frequently, and expect a very good crop this season.

Sweet potatoes: Sweet potatoes, planted last May, are currently under cultivation. Based on our previous experience, we are planting in beds, using drainage ditches, and fertilizing with TSP, potash, and urea. We are dipping the slips in aldrin before planting for worm control. Our last yield was 2 tons per acre, and we're hoping to top that with the current planting. Our second planting, in 1975, produced potatoes weighing 11 and 12 pounds. Since our crop of "better potatoes" was very fibrous, we are growing only sweet potatoes and yams at this time.

Bell yams: The first and second yam crops did not do very well. The third planting was therefore done in very rich soil, built up, and the current vines look very healthy.

Cassava processing: We are temporarily milling cassava in a mill designed by our workers, using materials we had around the project site. Once it is set up we will take our cassava to the government mill at Port Kaituma. We can grate 100 pounds of cassava in about three minutes using this homemade mill.

We collect bitter cassava from the field in open, 50 gallon

drums, and wash them in the trailer wagon through the jostling action on the way to the mill. The grater is a heavy table, 3′ x 8½′, with a hole 12″ x 14″ in the middle. Two iron pulleys welded together work the grater. The grater blade is made with a small three-cornered file, sharpened to make a small hole at half-inch intervals, with each row off-set to the last. We use a 5hp electric motor to turn the grater. One person puts the cassava in the grater, and another uses a cassava root to push the cassava against the grater.

Grated cassava comes through the bottom of the mill into a tub lined with a plastic feed bag. This is then lifted to the press, which consists of two heavy truck wheel rims, 21″ in diameter, with a solid bottom, except for a 2″ hole for the juice to escape. Cassava is pressed against the sides of a cylinder which has slits cut about 4″ apart and 6″ in length. In the bottom is a set of 5 ribs, made of crab wood, 2″ square with spacing to match. On these ribs is placed a lead cylinder to give better pressing effect.

The pressing plate is applied using a 10-ton hydraulic jack. It is set against a press frame made of wood timber. The cassava water drains into buckets and sits for about 30 minutes to let the starch settle to the bottom. The water is poured off into cooking vats and then boiled slowly for a few hours. It is strained through cheesecloth, then slowly boiled again until cooked down to a heavy syrup called *cassareep*. This is used in cooking as flavoring. The starch is also used in cooking, and to starch clothes.

The pressed cassava is put back through the grater and ground again, then dried on the floor. It is now about 40% of its original weight, and is mixed into pig feed. About 1,000 pounds of cassava produces 170 oz. of cassareep; 100 pounds of cassava will make 50 cassava breads, 18″ in diameter.

We have grated and pressed sweet potatoes by the same process as the cassava, producing a substance slightly sweeter than cassareep. We dried the processed potato. Some of the Guyanese have used it for porridge, which they said was very good. We have also produced a sweet potato flour which, mixed with eggs and fried in small cakes, has a meat-like flavor. It could easily be used as a meat stretcher. It can also be stored for periods of time in this flour state.

194

GARDEN CROPS

In addition to the major crops, we grow all the vegetables we need for the settlers, including cucumbers, bora beans, cabbage, lettuce, and others. They are all doing well.

FRUIT ORCHARD

We are developing a fruit orchard including many fruit trees native to Guyana. The trees are healthy and bearing well, though the fruits are still small because the trees are young. Our citrus orchard includes about 3,500 to 4,000 trees. We are also growing extremely healthy, fast-growing cashew trees.

Pineapples: Pineapples are thriving alongside the road leading into Jonestown. Because suckers were not available at the time of our first planting, we planted tops which we collected wherever we could find them. From our first crop we planted 600 suckers. Being large in size, these suckers quickly produced, but the fruit was small. We are now planting only small suckers or tops, which will delay the fruit for a year or two, but should produce larger sized pineapples. A third crop of 1,000 suckers was planted, and another crop of 1,000 is ready. We expect to produce beyond our own need in the near future.

Bananas: We are harvesting an average of 2,000 pounds of bananas each month. We first planted approximately 3,500 banana suckers in a mile stretch alongside the road into Jonestown. We discovered that plantings done in the rainy season did not come up, and only those planted in windrows would last. We have not used an insecticide to date, relying instead on ash from the burning and rotting wood to reduce the incidence of insects. This combination has also served to fertilize, so we have added fertilizer only once in nearly three years. Three delicious varieties of banana are bearing: apple, cayanne, and fig, plus plantain. A propagation field has been developed for rapid growth of suckers. We have started a few dwarf cayenne trees and five black banana suckers.

EXPERIMENTING

Experiments with garden crops are conducted to test non-commercial fertilizers, utilizing ingredients "produced" at the project site. Onions, and some legumes such as mung beans, are examples of crops under experimental cultivation. We are also growing coffee. Sea shells, manure, and compost are distributed on one acre plots in 2 ton, 4 ton, and 6 ton quantities. Results show how much fertilizer is needed for best growing conditions. Long garden rows are measured for best proportion to the acre.

Generally, experience has shown that cultivars are acclimating, growing stronger with each crop. For example, the star-leaf sweet potato took seven months to harvest the first time it was planted. The last crop was ready for harvest in only 3-4 months, and some, the size of medium-sized grapefruit, were ready in 2 months.

Cutlass beans: In the face of warnings from some local people that the cutlass bean would make people sick, we have successfully cultivated it and turned it into delicious foodstuffs. The government analysis station in Georgetown reported it was a good source of protein. We also use it for stock and animal feed and green manure. If we have enough seeds, we roast them for excellent snacks. The vine, which is also high in protein, is used for animals only at this time, but we expect to develop recipes using it for the settlers as well. Its excellent qualities were discovered when someone "took a chance" and ate it. It is a particularly valuable crop because it will grow anywhere, any time, and in any weather, requiring only one weeding and little fertilizer.

A HOMEMADE PLANTER

Using odds and ends from around the project site, like bicycle sprockets and chain, we created a mechanical planter that enabled us to plant 5 acres in an 8-hour day. We have since then converted our spring-tooth cultivator into a planter that covered the 5 acres in 3½ hours, using one driver and four other people. This job previously took 20-60 workers 3 to 5 days to complete.

Here's how we did it: We reset the cultivator tines to match the furrows made by the wheel. Then we made a seat of boards that sits on top of the cultivator, large enough to hold four people at one time. Three-foot hoses are connected to the tines at one end, and to funnels made with cut-off plastic bleach bottles at the other end. The seeds are dropped through the funnels and the hoses to a pan set on the tines, from which they are dropped to the furrows. Another tine then follows to cover the furrows. The planter addition can be removed in one piece when the cultivator is needed for its usual purpose.

We similarly fashioned a homemade corn shaker, using wooden frames with mesh screens to shake the corn so we can clean out broken pieces of cob.

Jonestown School

In Jonestown education is a way of life which affects all aspects of life. It is our intent to make education relevant to the growth and maturity of the child physically, morally, socially, intellectually, artistically, and finally with the goal of guiding the child in the acquisition of habits, attitudes and skills such as will enable the child to participate in collective thought, values and activities.

PRE-SCHOOL

Nursery school children receive guidance, supervision of activities, and instruction. Most activities are group activities. Children are encouraged to participate. Curriculum includes learning the use of table utensils, cleanliness and health habits, number concepts, naming quantities, alphabet recognition, and dance routines with educational themes. Learning tools include manipulative toys, puzzles, individual chalkboards, and motor and perceptual motor facilities in the play yard to be described later.

ELEMENTARY EDUCATION

At present the Jonestown School includes grades 1 through 7. Classes are not organized by grade or age, but rather by ability. The child can progress as rapidly as he/she desires and is advanced to a higher ability grouping when the teacher determines that the child is able to perform with the next ability grouping. For example, we now have an eight-year-old child working on a level equivalent to that of two thirteen-year-old students.

The groupings currently in use are: pre-reading, elementary reading skills and moderate competency, and those with moderate to well-developed reading skills. However, reading skills are not exclusive. A basic phonetic approach is started,

197

accompanied by auditory training. The goal initially is to shift emphasis from phonetic analysis to sight reading as soon as phonetic analysis competency is achieved. Also, structural analysis, configuration and content skills are taught. At less advanced levels perceptual skills are stressed: visual, audio, tactile, motor and perceptual-motor skills which are fundamental to academic skills.

The school curriculum presently includes: language arts, receptive and expressive language which includes reading, writing, spelling and composition skills, mathematics, physical and earth science, social science (with emphasis on Guyanese history and culture), political science, and arts, crafts and music.

An emphasis is placed on development of educational games, activities, and materials utilizing materials indigenous to this area and parts of discarded objects. For example, many games, puzzles, and activities have been developed using local woods. Many individual chalkboards are used in place of paper and pencils. Chalkboards are usually made from steel plate with chalkboard paint covering. They are handy because pre-developed lessons can be secured to the chalkboard with the use of small magnets. Miniature chalkboards are also used for structural analysis, syllabication, prefix, root and suffix study and math fact drill cards, as everything can be wiped off and the boards re-used. Workbooks and paper lessons are done with the use of a plastic sheet cover and a wax lead marker. In this way the paper supplies and lessons can be re-used many times.

THE PLAY AREA

The children's playground at Jonestown is considered a vital educational tool as well as serving its traditional role as recreation. The playground includes many facilities designed to enhance basic body movement and balance skills as well as strength. The play items (which incidentally were designed by the Jonestown teacher and built by the children) include: a rolling barrel with an axle on pillow blocks, a great balance-developing device which rolls as the child "walks it"; a twenty foot stationary balance beam; a fifteen foot swinging balance beam; a bucking barrel designed to buck like a horse when the attached ropes are pulled from the sides; a twenty foot overhead ladder; double rings and trapeze bar; an acrobat bar (chinning bar) and two tether ball set-ups. Supplies also include basketballs, volleyballs, and nets, kickballs, soccer balls, baseball bats and accessories, badminton, and football. Central to the use of all equipment is the emphasis on cooperation rather than competitive values on the playground. Children are encouraged to help each other in performing various tasks on the playground.

THE WORK–STUDY CONCEPT

Students are involved in more than just "school" work in Jonestown. They are actively involved in the development and maintenance of Jonestown. Each child is required with help to care for his/her clothing, bedding, and living space and to participate in cleaning activities including domestic and yard and grounds care. Children even take some responsibility for maintenance of flower and plant beds and lawn care.

Also, on a merit basis, good workers are allowed to participate in the numerous work projects underway. Those who become conscientious, productive workers are frequently given the privilege of assisting with special projects. Indeed, the playground was one such project. Students helped collect, carry, debark the logs and poles and assisted with the construction. *(Note: This synopsis of the Jonestown School does not include a description of the vocational and technical training provided for young men and women beyond the seventh grade. In the fall, other academic training for older youth will begin.)*

Medical Facility

In Jonestown we are in the process of developing an efficient medical clinic. We presently have a doctor and two licensed medical practitioners, one in neuro-surgical specialty and the other in pediatrics. We also have six registered nurses and a doctor of pharmacology with experience in teaching.

Preventive medical care is emphasized. Physical examinations are given each 6 months to everyone in Jonestown with special attention to bimonthly well-baby checkups, pre-natal care and follow-up for those with chronic diseases such as diabetes mellitus and epilepsy. A dietician supervises the kitchen aided by one of the registered nurses who prepares therapeutic diets and maintains a high nutritional standard in the meals served.

Therapeutic vitamins are provided for all of the local children who were malnourished before coming to Jonestown. Those with anemic disorders have been treated with supplemental iron preparation. Such treatment has been effective in treating many of the children of this area.

Our clinic is becoming well-stocked and we are prepared at all times to give first aid.

Communal Kitchen

One of the first buildings one sees when traveling up the road to Jonestown is the all-purpose kitchen where meals and treats are provided to workers and residents there.

THE KITCHEN

Three complete wood-paneled walls are designed to make the best use of space, working materials and comfort, including large shelved and divided cabinets and drawers above and below the glassy-varnished spacious counters. Commercial refrigeration and freezer units are used to store perishable items (when other means of food preservation cannot be used). Food is stocked to the maximum with edibles from all the basic food groups including meats and proteins, starches and all varieties of succulent fruits and vegetables. Our kitchen has an ice-making unit, two cooking stoves (gas and kerosene) and a large, triple sectioned sink. Water comes from a hand-dug well that never runs dry all year long. It provides water for cooking, drinking, cleaning, laundry, and bathing for all Jonestown facilities.

The front wall of the kitchen is a full length serving counter having large removable partitions which can be raised or lowered at the servers' convenience to allow food to be served while reducing the entrance of insects to the kitchen itself. Such screening allows for the entrance of bright and healthy sunlight, while maintaining sanitation standards.

A large work table is secured in the middle of the floor under which airtight, water-resistant drums contain sugar, oil, various grains, and flour. Heavy duty pots of all sizes hang from the center ceiling. A large variety of kitchen utensils are stocked in the kitchen (including knives made in our metal workshop, providing all types of useful cutting edges).

A large, Guyanese-style wood oven is used for our massive bread-baking during the drier season. Cassava flour is one of the basic ingredients used in our bread.

Menus: Menus are planned in advance to allow for food supplying areas to be filled and for the medical staff to check for maximum nutritional health and vitamin standards to be maintained. Almost all foods are home-grown and home-prepared. The kitchen is an organized center of activity almost 24 hours a day as work teams prepare for the next day's meals, or bag lunches for workers further removed from the central dining area in their day's work. Working in shifts on a team basis has been found to be the most efficient method and also allows for ample rest for all participants and maximum use of all materials.

Meals: Meals are always promptly served. Breakfast is served in three shifts. First, the outdoor workers eat from 5:40 to 6:30 am, then the senior citizens eat from 7:00 to 7:30 and finally the children eat from 7:30 to 8:00 am. Naturally allowances are made for seniors or for any ill persons to have their meals served to them in their residences. Breakfast menus include such foods as eggs from Jonestown chickens, cooked cereals, pancakes and homemade syrup and varying fruits seasonally available. Biscuits, rolls, and breads are baked daily by the cooking staff.

Many lunches are pre-made for workers and are distributed at breakfast time. The bulk of lunches utilize sandwiches made of cutlass bean patty, fish patty, peanut butter, egg salad, fried egg, eggplant, or pork meat products. Nuts, fruits, pastries or cookies are added as desserts. These are eaten at sheltered spots right on the work site. Seniors and children are served a hot meal in the communal dining room.

The kitchen also works closely with the nursing department to prepare calorie-rich, nourishing snacks and drinks in the mid-morning and mid-afternoon for children and underweight individuals. Those who are overweight are encouraged to take advantage of low-calorie meals, especially dished up by our medical staff.

Our cooking staff is comprised of an RN (who once managed an

Italian restaurant), and a number of experienced individuals of all ages and the menu planning reflects their various cultural and ethnic backgrounds, as well as incorporating all local foods and products they have absorbed from the Amerindian adaptation of local products.

Kitchen cleanup crews work on a rotating schedule. Each person carries out his/her specific duties in a quiet, efficient manner. The dishes are cold-water rinsed, washed and stacked, then washed in a soapy detergent with bleach and boiling water, and put away. The cleaning process is carried on during and after kitchen activities. All surfaces are continually scrubbed and sanitized from ceiling to floor to provide the most healthful environment.

Afterword

The agricultural project has been financed entirely by members of Peoples Temple. Valuable in-kind services have been provided by the Guyana government on a number of occasions. We could never have progressed so far so fast were it not for the total cooperation given by the Guyanese at every step of the way.

We look forward to a relationship of friendship and mutual support between our mission settlers and Guyanese from every walk of life. We can only express our appreciation by trying to make our experiences useful for others engaged in similar efforts to expand and improve cultivation and development of the rich interior of Guyana, with the goal of benefiting her people.

Father Divine's Song of Retribution

THE FOLLOWING POEM was sung—along with other adoring praises—to Father Divine.

I am the grim reaper, Retribution,
Whom all men should terribly fear!
I seek the godless in sure visitation
And destroy the wicked both far and near.

I am the law of retributive justice.
Who now shall escape my command?
I hold the destiny of my critics
In the hollow of my mighty hand.

I am vengeance, the rewarder of crime,
Punishing the blasphemers against God's Name.
I curse them to the very end of time,
For not believing in the Lord's Holy Reign.

I am the administrator of equity,
The accuser of men's polluted lives;
I am the judge of their iniquity,
The persecutor without compromise.

With my deadly sickle in hand,
I am reaping on the left and the right.
Righteousness shall rule in every man
Or Retribution shall destroy his birthright!

Executions, fire and loss,
Beatings and murders appointed to be,
Cosmic disasters and death are the costs
Of retributive justice on land, air and sea.

Moses and Jude and the prophets of old
Wrote of hate and strife and ungodly crimes;
Of Justice and Judgment they all foretold
And revealed the curses in those olden times.

Thus treachery and strife and irreligious hate
Mark the reaping of all my critics the same;
Not one has escaped his retributional fate,
For the grim reaper, God, Father Divine, compensates!

Martin E. Marty's Reaction

IN A PERCEPTIVE afterthought to Jonestown, Martin Marty of the *Christian Century* magazine focused on the tendency of religionists to seek to restore authority by totalitarian tactics.

Why Conservative Cults Are Growing

IF ALL the recent unsolicited *Escape from Freedom* articles that came to this magazine over the transom were piled atop each other, they would not fit over the transom.

By *Escape from Freedom* essays we refer to all those that urge mainline church people to win back their youth by pushing discipline, submission, authoritarianism, denial of choice. In other words, those that tout the ways of the various superintensive groups, be they religious or secular, Christian or not. By *Escape from Freedom* pieces we imply those which urge mainline congregations to win back families to loyalty by copying the fundamentalist modes that teach total womanhood through total submission to a lord and master-husband. Or those that urge mainline church people to overcome basic youth conflicts by having youth accept hierarchy, living under a totalitarian divine Father who dominates an authoritarian earthly father who holds in submission an authoritative mother.

By *Escape from Freedom* articles we imply those that misuse Dean Kelley's famed *Why Conservative Churches Are Growing* and tell milder denominations to emulate Jehovah's Witnesses, the earlier Black Muslims, and other groups which, because they adhere to the absolutist/fanatic/zealous/conformist pattern, do prosper.

Escape from Freedom essays also misuse John Murray Cuddihy's argument in *No Offense* in order to chip away at the idea of civility in religion. They would replace it with nostalgia for Good Old Days when people believed enough to go on crusades or instigate inquisitions. We also refer to the capitulations by weary liberal academicians to the illiberal diseases of the day.

The tragic victims of totalist cultism who died with the Peoples Temple in Guyana may not have died wholly in vain if they teach others to remodel visions of discipleship and order. (Let reaction *not* take the form of legal repression, which is unconstitutional and unjust and unproductive, since it adds to the lure of suspect and suffering groups!) The Temple people lived out the final logic of submission and followership; perhaps their end may caution some would-be converts to hyperintensive groups to take care before they traipse along behind slouching new messiahs. If the Jonesian example leads some scholars who had been hungering for authoritarianism to stop asking others to follow these ways, our transom will be less clogged.

Oh, that our mail slot may overflow with needed articles of the opposite sort: on how to teach people to live in a crowded and armed world, a world in which we must combine conviction with civility, commitment with empathy, discipleship in the group with risk in the world. We are cheered to see some Born-Again and Pentecostal folk moving into this Phase Two. It is ironic to see some mainliners pass them in the aisle, going the other way.

Yes, we have read biblical texts that call us to leave all behind for the sake of a yoke. But it is the yoke not of a Lord with an insecure ego who demands mastery but one who said, "The Son of man came not to be served but to serve.

. . . " Is John 8:36 a call to escape from freedom, to build high walls and dig trenches for huddling: "If the Son makes you free, you will be free indeed"?

Whoever henceforth sends us *Escape from Freedom* articles should know that they will be reposed no longer in the file marked "Bouille Chitte." We now have another. Marked "Dangerous."

Martin E. Marty.

Statement of the General Minister of the Disciples of Christ

ON MARCH 12, 1979, the general minister of the Disciples of Christ issued the following statement, which represents an attempt to come to terms with the denomination's relationship with Jim Jones and People's Temple. Thorough discussion and debate of its various assumptions and arguments might well be the most practical way of getting at the issues of the church and Jonestown. The statement was made to the administrative committee of the denomination's general board. The full statement follows.

March 12, 1979

I want to report to you on the tragedy of Jonestown relative to our structure and relationships, and offer you my recommendations.

Some 48 hours after the tragedy—even before the scope of it was fully known—I issued a statement of concern for the families of the victims and for survivors, and acknowledged the relationship of both the congregation and its pastor to the Disciples of Christ.

At the same time, I took what I felt to be an appropriate step of getting the question of denominational followup action out of the hands of staff and into the hands of those who initiate and make policy. Because of the questions being raised as to what the Disciples were planning to do about People's Temple, I indicated that I would make an inquiry with the legislative bodies of the church whether there ought to be a procedure for disavowing congregations, a procedure which we have never had.

The recent dissolving of People's Temple makes the specific question moot. But the issue remains. Does this church have an obligation to itself, to other Christians, and to society to institute a procedure of disassociation from congregations that run amuck?

If fanatical fringe groups can enhance their credibility by aligning themselves with major denominations, the ministry and mission and witness of all mainstream Protestantism suffers. The anti-religionists tried more than once on national television following Jonestown to make the point that People's Temple was not a cult but a part of the Christian mainstream.

There is the church-state issue involved as well. The government would like to close the tax loopholes which cults and pseudo-religious bodies can take advantage of. We have come to the point where government is beginning to define what constitutes a church, and what appropriate church activities are. We believe this to be an infringement on the First Amendment protection of religion.

So, I bring to you, as I indicated I would, the matter of whether we have a weakness in structure that endangers Christian witness and mission. Let me share with you my own observations and recommendations.

First, whatever we do, *let us act with the good of humanity in mind, and not the reputation of the church.* We are concerned with people and ministry. We are concerned with love and compassion. We are here to save the world, and not the institution, even when the institution is the church. As great a tragedy as Jonestown was, we should not act precipitantly with our self-protection as the motivation.

Second, *having a policy to disavow congregations probably could not have foretold or averted Jonestown.* People's Temple, until at some point near the end, behaved much like many other congregations with a strong devotion to their pastors. In any case, it is unlikely that the church would have used a disavowal procedure against an entire congregation, having no comprehension that strange behavior by a pastor and complaints of mistreatment by members was the prelude to mass murder and suicide. We have developed responsible policies and criteria for the order of ministry in the Christian Church (Disciples of Christ) and those policies were operative concerning the standing of Jones at the time of the tragedy.

Third, *just as we ask the individual prospective member only if she or he believes in Jesus Christ, we offer relationship to congregations on the same basis, and accept on faith the reply in each case.* Recognition is achieved by action of the congregation and the endorsement of the region. The covenantal relationship thus formed with the whole church is one of mutual support and accountability. Let God be the judge of deviation from the gospel. And society judge violations of the civil law.

Fourth, *it is not so much a body of common beliefs that binds us together as Disciples of Christ but an understanding of the church as one.* Historically we have said the church of Jesus Christ on earth is essentially, intentionally and constitutionally one. In tolerating and welcoming difference of opinion, we leave ourselves no measuring rod by which errancy can be determined. A congregation can be a part of us because it believes the church is one.

Fifth, *the social witness, which got Jim Jones interested in the Disciples in the first place, should not be lost by the church because opponents tie it to the aberrations of Jones.* Let me share with you part of a letter that appeared in the Indianapolis Star: "As one who is not a member of the Disciples of Christ, but who has observed for a long time their deep concern for the minorities in our land, I would like to express my sympathy to their leaders and members over the recent painful events in Guyana. It is my hope that the tragic events over which we all agonize will not discourage that denomination in continuing to be sensitive to the needs of the spiritually and socially disinherited among us. By affirming ecumenical vision the Disciples of Christ have won the admiration of us all."

And last, *if we have shortcomings in connection with our congregations and ministry, it is at the point of shepherding, not*

210

policing. Perhaps the most significant decision we Disciples made in the restructure period of the sixties was to recognize ourselves as a covenant church. We are still learning what that means. The covenant concept takes seriously the New Testament image of the church as "the body of Christ." It recognizes the organic unity of the body. By God's design the parts of the body are dependent on one another. They "care for one another. If one member suffers, all suffer together; if one member is honored, all rejoice together." To say that we are in a covenantal relationship is to say that, in Christ, we are responsible for one another as members of any living body are. In practical terms, this means that in the Christian Church, we sense the interdependence of various structural manifestations of the body—congregation, region and general organization. These parts not only serve and support one another but also rely on one another. This relationship is described in part in paragraph 83 of The Design:

> As part of the Christian Church (Disciples of Christ) congregations share creatively in its total mission of witness and service. Equally, the Christian Church (Disciples of Christ) in its general and regional manifestations sustains its congregations through its commitment to their welfare and needs. Thus, concern for the integrity of each manifestation is shared and witness is given to the interrelatedness of the whole church.

We need to amplify the meaning of this covenantal relationship through a closer relationship among our congregations, all of them, not just those that ask for denominational services. We have a responsibility to visit and nurture them, just as congregations have a responsibility to visit and nurture their members. I have recently proposed to the Conference of Regional Ministers and Moderators that the Conference be responsible for encouraging all regions to develop consistent procedures in applying the policies and criteria we have adopted for the order of ministry in matters of candidacy, licensing, ordination and ministerial standing. The regions will be encouraged to establish ways and means for at least annual visits to every congregation regardless of its size and degree of participation. The regions will be asked to encourage all persons who hold ministerial standing to report annually on the ministry in which they are involved. This will enable the regions to be faithful to their responsibility for maintaining standards; assist in maintaining accountability and contact; help in the development of a comprehensive and accurate picture of the region's total ministry and provide a basis for support. The General Board committee on ministerial standing which is responsible for certifying the standing of persons engaged in non-regional ministries will be asked to develop specific procedures to apply when persons assume positions outside the boundaries of our regularly constituted regions and are not related to any of our denominational organizations or ecumenical bodies with which we have official relationships. Our aim as a church is and ought to be to accept responsibility for, and accountability to, one another as we seek to carry out God's mission.

Therefore, it is my recommendation to this Administrative Committee of the General Board that the Christian Church (Disciples of Christ) reaffirm its commitment to the covenantal relationship which binds us together as a church, and to congregational freedom, taking no action that would involve passing judgment on a congregation's ministry, and that we continue to develop new and creative ways for shepherding congregations and encouraging them to accept and live in a relationship of mutual support with other congregations in their region and in the whole church. I would further recommend that we reaffirm our commitment to the two priorities established by the Kansas City General Assembly—to extend human rights and to renew congregational life and witness. It is my hope that all of the tragedies of the human family will be seen in the context ot God's ultimate triumph.

The Tape

AFTER COMPLETING THE body of this book I had an opportunity
to listen to a tape recording that purports to represent the
voice of James Jones and his followers and the cries of
children and others during the last moments in Jonestown.
I am a person who is more audio than visual—that is, I
judge more by what I hear with my ears than by what I see
through a pair of rather poor eyes. The tape corresponded
substantially to the transcript that follows. That transcript
first appeared in the *New York Times* on March 15, 1979.
After listening to the tape, I checked with an acquaintance
in the television industry to be sure that the voice on the
tape was actually that of Jim Jones. Elaborate tests with
voice experts confirmed that the voice was almost surely
his. The tape had been edited, of what I do not know. I was
led to believe that the most responsible act would be to
include in this appendix the transcript as published by the
New York Times. The *New York Times* prefaced its publication
by stating that "sources who are familiar with investigations of the Peoples Temple have indicated that the
contents of this tape are identical with portions of the
Government-held tape that have been disclosed over the
last few months." Reading will hardly convey the
impression that listening provides. It is of a man
substantially in control of a multitude to the point that even
when confronted with a sensible effort to stop the carnage
he is able at once to rally the crowd against the brave

woman protestor and at the same time to act as her protector after she has been threatened by the crowd. One hears on the tape Jones's control over the lives of both black and white followers. One hears a reiteration of the conflict over John-John Stoen. (One wonders who Ejar is. Is it another name for the young Stoen child?) One hears, too, the ambiguity surrounding the final events. Did Jones decree the carnage at Kaituma airstrip—the doom of the congressman and the others? Or was he simply a passive witness of the acting out of pathologies on the part of his inner circle of guards and followers?

I have talked with others who hear in the tape things I do not hear, and because the tape itself is merely at this writing "purported," I shall not attempt to claim for it the status of evidence. The suspicion must be that it will ultimately be revealed as authentic and that the largely quiet conversational, but sometimes nagging and petulant, voice on the tape is that of a man who was capable over the years of making hundreds and hundreds of people believe that death with him was preferable to life without him. It is the mutest of testimonies to a world in which values—even truth itself—are torn from their moorings, leaving in their path a debris of superstition (secular or religious—it does not matter), paranoia, and will toward death. The transcript follows.

Excerpts From Transcript of a Purported Tape of Final Moments Jonestown

Following are excerpts from a transcript of a tape recording obtained by The New York Times from the International Home Video Club Inc. of New York. It purports to be a recording of the final 43 minutes of the mass deaths at Jonestown, Guyana, last Nov. 18, in which the followers of the

Rev. Jim Jones died. Sources who are familiar with investigations of the People's Temple have indicated that the contents of this tape are identical with portions of the Government-held tape that have been disclosed over the last few months.

JONES: I've tried my best to give you a good life.

In spite of all that I've tried, a handful of our people, with their lies, have made our life impossible. There's no way to detach ourself from what's happened today.

Not only are we in a compound situation; not only are there those who have left and committed the betrayal of the century; some have stolen children from others and they are in pursuit right now to kill them, because they stole their children. And we are sitting here waiting on a powder keg.

So, to sit here and wait for the catastrophe that's going to happen on that airplane—it's going to be a catastrophe. It almost happened here. Almost happened when the Congressman was nearly killed here. You can't steal people's children. You can't take off with people's children without expecting a violent reaction. And that's not so unfamiliar to us, either, even if we—even if we were Judeo-Christian—if we weren't Communists. The world opinion suffers violence and the violent shall take it by force. If we can't live in peace then let's die in peace. [Applause.]

We've been so betrayed. We have been so terribly betrayed. [Music and singing.]

What's going to happen here in a matter of a few minutes is that one of those people on that plane is going to shoot the pilot—I know that. I didn't plan it, but I know it's going to happen. They're gonna shoot that pilot and down comes that plane into the jungle. And we had better not have any of our children left when it's over. Because they'll parachute in here on us.

I'm going to be just as plain as I know how to tell you. I've never lied to you. I never have lied to you. I know that's what's gonna happen. That's what he intends to do; and he will do it. He'll do it.

What's with being so bewildered with many, many pressures on my brain seeing all people behave so treasonous—there was just too much for me to put together. But I now know what he was telling me. And it'll happen. If the plane gets in the air even.

So my opinion is that you be kind to children, and be kind to seniors, and take the potion like they used to take in Ancient Greece, and step over quietly; because we are not committing suicide—it's a revolutionary act. We can't go back; they won't leave us alone. They're now going back to tell more lies, which means more Congressmen. And there's no way, no way we can survive.

Anybody. Anyone that has any dissenting opinion, please speak. Yes. You can have an opportunity, but if the children are left, we're going to have them butchered. We can make a strike, but we'll be striking against people that we don't want to strike against. We'd like to get the people who caused this stuff; and some—if some people here are prepared and know how to do that, to go in town and get Timothy Stoen, but there's no plane. There's no plane. You can't catch a plane in time.

'They'll Not Take Our Death in Vain'

He's responsible for it. He brought these people to us. He and Deanna Myrtle. The people in San Francisco will not—not be idle. Or would they? They'll not take our death in vain, you know. Yes.

WOMAN: Is it too late for Russia?

JONES: At this point, it's too late for Russia. They killed. They started to kill. That's why it makes it too late for Russia. Otherwise, I'd say, yes, sir, you bet your life. But it's too late. I can't control these people. They're out there. They've gone with the guns. And it's too late. And once we kill anybody—at least, that's the way I've always—I've always put my lot with you. If one of my people do something, that's me.

And they say I don't have to take the blame for this—but I don't live that way. They said, deliver up Ejar; we tried to get the man back here. Ejar, whose mother's been lying on him, and lying on him, and trying to break up this family. And they've all agreed to kill us by any means necessary. Do you think I'm going to deliver them Ejar? Not on your life.

MAN: I know a way to find Stoen if it'll help us.

JONES: No. You're not going. You're not going.

216

You're not going. I can't live that way. I cannot live that way. I've lived with—for all; I'll die for all. [Applause.]

I've been living on hope for a long time, Christine and I appreciate—you've always been a very good agitator. I like agitation because you have to see two sides of one issue— two sides of a question.

But what those people are gonna get done; and what they get through will make our lives worse than hell. Will make us—will make the rest of us not accept it. When they get through lying.

They posed so many lies between there and that truck that we are—we are done in as far as any other alternative.

WOMAN: Well, I say let's make an air—airlift to Russia. That's what I say. I don't think nothing is impossible, if you believe it.

JONES: How are we going to do that? How are you going to airlift to Russia?

WOMAN: Well, I thought they said if we got in an emergency, they gave you a code to let them know.

JONES: No, they didn't. They gave us a code that they'd let us know on that issue; not us create an issue for them. They said that we—if they saw the country coming down they'd give us a code. They'd give us a code. We can check on that and see if it's on the code. Did you check with Russia to see if they'll take us in a minute but otherwise we die?

I don't know what else to say to these people. But to me death is not a fearful thing. It's living that's cursed. I have never, never, never, never seen anything like this before in my life. I've never seen people take the law and do —in their own hands and provoke us and try to purposely agitate mother of children. There is no need to finish us; it's not worth living like this. Not worth living like this.

WOMAN: I think that there were too few who left for 1,200 people to give them their lives for those people that left.

JONES: Do you know how many left?

WOMAN: Oh, 20-odd. That's a small—

JONES: Some 20-odd.

WOMAN: Compared to what's here.

'What's Gonna Happen?'

JONES: 20-odd. But what's gonna happen when they don't leave? I hope that they

217

could leave. But what's gonna happen when they don't leave?

WOMAN: You mean the people here?

JONES: Yeah, what's going to happen to us when they don't leave, when they get on the plane and the plane goes down?

WOMAN: I don't think they'll go down.

JONES: You don't think they'll go down? I wish I could tell you was right—but I'm right. There's one man there who blames, and rightfully so, Judy Blakey for the murder— for the murder of his mother, and he'll—he'll stop that pilot by any means necessary. He'll do it. That plane'll come out of the air. There's no way you fly a plane without a pilot.

WOMAN: I wasn't speaking about that plane. I was speaking about a plane for us to go to Russia.

JONES: How—To Russia? You think Russia's gonna want—no—You think Russia's gonna want us with all this stigma? We had some value, but now we don't have any value.

WOMAN: Well I don't see it like that. I mean, I feel like that—as long as there's life there's hope. That's my faith.

JONES: Well, some—everybody dies. Some place that hope runs out; because everybody dies. I haven't seen anybody yet didn't die. And I like to choose my own kind of death for a change. I'm tired of being tormented to hell, that's what I'm tired of. Tired of it. [Applause.]

To have other people's lives in my hands, and I certainly don't want your life in my hands. I'm going to tell you, Christine, without me, life has no meaning. [Applause.] I'm the best thing you'll ever have.

I want—want—I have to pay—I'm standing with [inaudible]. I'm standing with those people. They're part of me. I could detach myself—my attorney says, detach myself. No, no, no, no, no, no. I never detach myself from any of your troubles. I've always taken your troubles right on my shoulders. And I'm not going to change that now. It's too late. I've been running too long. Not going to change now. [Applause.]

Maybe the next time you'll get to go to Russia. The next time round. This is—what I'm talking about now is the dispensation of judgment. This is a revolutionary—a revolutionary suicide council. I'm not talking about self—self-destruction. I'm talking about what we have no other road. I will take your call; we will put it to the Russians. And I can tell you the answer now, because I'm a prophet. Call the Russians and tell them and see if they'll take us.

WOMAN: I said I'm not ready to die.

JONES: I don't think you are.

WOMAN: But I know what you meant.

JONES: I don't think you are.

WOMAN: But I look at all the babies and I think they deserve to live.

JONES: But don't they deserve much more—they deserve peace.

WOMAN: We all came here for peace.

JONES: And we've—have we had it?

WOMAN: No.

JONES: I tried to give it to you. I've laid down my life, practically. I've practically died every day to give you peace. And you still not have any peace. You look better than I've seen you in a long while but it's still not the kind of peace that I want to give you.

WOMAN: I know that. But I still think, as an individual, I have a right to—

JONES: You do, and I'm listening.

WOMAN: —to say what I think, what I feel. And I think we all have a right to our own destiny as individuals.

JONES: Right.

WOMAN: And I think I have a right to choose mine and everybody else has a right to choose theirs.

JONES: Yes. I'm not criticizing.

WOMAN: Well I think I still have a right to my own opinion.

JONES: I'm not taking it from you. I'm not taking it from you.

'Your Life Has Been Extended'

MAN: Christine, you're only standing here because he was here in the first place. So I don't know what you're talking about, having an individual life. Your life has been extended to the day that you're standing there because of him.

JONES: I guess she has as much right to speak as anybody else to. What did you say, Ruby? [Voice.] Well you'll regret that, this very day if you don't die. You'll regret it if you do though you don't die. You'll regret it.

JONES: I saved them. I saved them, but I made my example. I made my expression. I made my manifestation and the world was ready, not ready for me. Paul said I was a man born out of due season. I've been born out of due season, just like all we are—and the best testimony we can make is to leave this goddamn world. [Applause.]

WOMAN: You must prepare to die.

WOMAN: I'm not talking to her. Will you let—would you let her or let me talk?

JONES: Keep talking.

WOMAN: Would you make her sit down and let me talk while I'm on the floor or let her talk.

JONES: How can you tell the leader what to do if you live. I've listened to you. You asked me about Russia. I'm right now making a call to Russia. What more do you suggest? I'm listening to you. You've yet to give me one slight bit of encouragement. I just now . . . to go there and do that.

[Voices.]

JONES: Everybody hold it. We didn't come—hold it. Hold it. Hold it. Hold it.

[Voices.]

JONES: Lay down your burdens. I'm gonna lay down my burden. Down by the riverside. Shall we lay them down here by the side of Guyana? No man didn't take our lives. Right now. They haven't taken them. But when they start parachuting out of the air, they'll seek some of our innocent babies. I'm not—I don't want . . . They've got to shoot me to get through to some of these people. I'm not telling them take your child. Can you let them take your child? [Voices: No. No. No.]

JONES: I want to see [Lots of voices.] Please, please, please, please, please, please, please.

MAN: I'm ready to go. If you tell us we have to give our lives now, we're ready—all the rest of the sisters and brothers are with me.

JONES: Some months I've tried to keep this thing from happening. But I now see it's the will—it's the will of Sovereign Being that this happened to us. That we lay down our lives in protest against what's been done.

That we lay down our lives to protest at what's being done. The criminality of people. The cruelty of people. Who walked out of here today. Do you know who walked out.

Mostly white people. [Voices.] Mostly white people walked.

I'm so grateful for the ones that didn't—those who knew who they are. I just know there's no point—there's no point to this. We are born before our time. They won't accept us. And I don't think we should sit here and take any more time for our children to be endangered; because if they come after our children, we give them our children, then our children will suffer forever.

WOMAN: [Unintelligible.]

JONES: What comes now, folks, what comes now.

MAN: Everybody hold it.

JONES: Say peace. Say peace. Say peace. Say peace. What's come. Don't let—Take Dwyer on down to the east house. Take Dwyer.

WOMAN: Everybody be quiet please.

MAN: That means sit down, sit down. Sit down.

'I Tried So Very, Very Hard'

JONES: They know. I tried so very, very hard. They're trying over here to see what's going to happen in Los Angeles. Who is he?

[Voices.]

JONES: Get Dwyer out of here before something hap-pens to him. Dwyer. I'm not talking about Ejar. I said Dwyer. Ain't nobody gonna take Ejar. I'm not lettin' 'em take Ejar.

WOMAN: At one time, I felt just like [inaudible], but after today I don't feel anything because the biggest majority of the people that left here for a fight and I know it really hurt my heart because—

JONES: Broke your heart, didn't it?

WOMAN: It broke my heart completely. All of this year the white people had been with us and they're not a part of us. So we might as well end it now; because I don't see [Music and voices.]

JONES: Well it's all over, all over. What a legacy, what a legacy. What's the Red Brigade doing, and one's that ever made any sense anyway? They invaded our privacy. They came into our home. They followed us 6,000 miles away. Red Brigade showed them justice. The Congressman's dead.

Please get us some medication. Simple. It's simple, there's no convulsions with it. It's just simple. Just, please, get it. Before it's too late. The G.D.F. will be here, I tell you, get movin', get movin', get movin'. [Voices.]

221

Don't be afraid to die. You'll see people land out here. They'll torture some of our children here. They'll torture our people. They'll torture our seniors. We cannot have this.

Are you going to separate yourself from whoever shot the Congressman? I don't know who shot him.

VOICES: No. No. No.

JONES: Let's make our peace. And those had a right to go, and they had a right to— how many are dead? Aw, God, Almighty God. Huh. Patty Park is dead? [Voices.]

WOMAN: Some of the others who are . . . long enough in a safe place to write about . . .

JONES: I don't know how in the world they're ever going to write about us. It's just too late. It's too late. The Congressman's dead. The . . . Many of our . . . are dead. They're all laying out there dead.

JONES: Please can we hasten? Can we hasten with our medication? You don't know what you've done. I tried. [Applause and music.]

JONES: They saw it happen and ran in the bush and dropped the machine guns. Never in my life. But there'll be more. But we've got to move. Are you gonna get that medica-

tion here? You've got to move. Approximately about 40 minutes.

WOMAN: Do . . . have to know when the people that are standing there in the aisles, go stand in the radio room yard, everybody get behind a table and back this way. O.K. There's nothing to worry about. Everybody keep calm; and try and keep your children calm. And all those children that help, let the little children in and reassure them. They're not crying from pain; it's just a little bitter-tasting, they're not crying out of any pain. Annie Miguel, can I please see you back . . .

'Sit Down and Be Quiet'

MAN: So much to do before I came here. So let me tell you about it. It might make a lot of you feel a little more comfortable. Sit down and be quiet, please.

One of the things that I used to do, I used to be a therapist. And the kind of therapy that I did had to do with reincarnation in past life situations. And every time anybody had an experience of going into a past life, I was fortunate enough through father to be able to let them experience it all the way

222

through their death, so to speak.

And everybody was so happy when they made that step to the other side.

WOMAN: I just want to say something for everyone that I see that is standing around, or crying. This is nothing to cry about. This is something we could all rejoice about. We could be happy about this. They always told us that we could cry when you're coming into this world. So we're leaving it, and we're leaving it peaceful, I think we should be—you should be happy about this. I was just thinking about Jim Jones. He just has suffered and suffered and suffered. We have the honor guard and we don't even have a chance to . . . here . . . one more chance. That's few that's gone. There's many more here . . . That's not all of us. That's not all, yet. That's just a few that have died. I'm looking at so many people crying. I wish you would not cry. [Applause.] I've been here one year and nine months. And I never felt better in my life. Not in San Francisco, but until I came to Jonestown. I had a . . . life. I had a beautiful life. I don't see nothing that I should be crying about. We should be happy. At least I am—[Applause.]

[Music.]

WOMAN: Good to be alive today. I just like to thank Dad, 'cause he was the only one that stood up for me when I needed him. And thank you, Dad.

WOMAN: I'm glad that you're my brothers and sisters. I'm glad to be here. [Voices.]

JONES: Please, for God's sake, let's get on with it. We've lived—we've lived as no other people lived and loved. We've had as much of this world as you're gonna get. Let's just be done with it. Let's be done with the agony of it. [Applause.]

JONES: It's far, far harder to have to walk through every day, die slowly—and from the time you're a child till the time you get gray, you're dying.

Dishonest, and I'm sure that they'll—they'll pay for it. They'll pay for it. This is a revolutionary suicide. This is not a self-destructive suicide. So they'll pay for this. They brought this upon us. And they'll pay for that. I leave that destiny to them.

[Voices.]

JONES: —wants to go with their child has a right to go with their child. I think it's humane.

I want to go—I want to see you go, though. They can take me and do what they want—whatever they want to do. I want to see you go. I don't want to see you go through this hell no more. No more. No more. No more.

We're trying. If everybody—relax. The best thing you do to relax and you won't have no problem. You'll have no problem with this thing. If you just relax.

MAN: —a great deal because it's Jim Jones. And the way the children are laying there now. I'd rather see them lay like that than to see them have to die like the Jews did, which was pitiful anyhow. And I just like to thank Dad, who give them this life, and also death. And I appreciate the fact the way our children are going. Because, like Dad said, when they come in, what they're going to do to our children—they're going to massacre our children.

And also the ones that they take capture, they're gonna just let them grow up and be dummies, like they want them to be. And not grow up to be a person like the one and only Jim Jones. So I'd like to thank dad for the opportunity for letting Jonestown be not what it could be, but what Jones-

town is. Thank you, Dad.
[Applause.]
MAN: It is not to be feared. It is not to be feared. It is a friend. It's a friend. Sitting there show your love for one another. Take your time—

JONES: Let's get gone. Let's get gone. Let's get gone. We had nothing we could do. We can't separate ourselves from our own people. For 20 years laying in some old rotten nursing home. Taking us through all these anguish years. They took us and put us in chains and that's nothing. This business—that business—there's no comparison to that, to this.

They've robbed us of our land and they've taken us and driven us and we tried to find ourselves. We tried to find a new beginning. But it's too late. You can't separate yourself from your brother and your sister. No way I'm going to do it. I refuse. I don't know who fired the shot. I don't know who killed the Congressman. But as far as I'm concerned I killed him. You understand what I'm saying. I killed him. He had no business coming. I told him not to come.

WOMAN: Right. Right.
[Music.]
[Children crying.]
JONES: I, with respect, die

with the beginning of dignity. Lay down your life with dignity. Don't lay down with tears and agony. It's nothing to death. It's like Mac said, it's just stepping over to another plane. Don't be this way. Stop this hysterics. This is not the way for people who are Socialists or Communists to die. No way for us to die. We must die with some dignity . . . we have no choice. Now we have some choice. Do you think they're gonna allow this to be done? And allow us to get by with this? You must be insane—children, it's just something to put you to rest. Oh God.

[Children crying.] Mother, mother, mother, mother, mother, please. Mother please. Please. Please. Don't do this. Don't do this. Lay down your life with your child. But don't do this.

Free at last. Keep—keep your emotions down. Keep your emotions down. Children, it will not hurt. If you'd be—if you be quiet. If you be quiet. [Music.] [Children crying.]

It's never been done before, you say. It's been done by every tribe in history. Every tribe facing annihilation. All the Indians of the Amazon are doing it right now. They refuse to bring any babies into the world. They kill every child that comes into the world. Because they don't want to live in this kind of a world.

Death 'A Million Times Preferable'

So be patient. Be patient. Death is—I tell you, I don't care how many screams you hear; I don't care how many anguished cries, death is a million times preferable to spend more days in this life. If you knew what was ahead of you—if you knew what was ahead of you, you'd be glad to be stepping over tonight.

Death, death, death is common to people. And the Eskimos, they take death in their stride. Let's be digni—let's be dignified. If you quit telling them they're dying—if you would also stop some of this nonsense—adults, adults, I call on you to stop this nonsense.

I call on you to quit exciting your children, when all they're doing is going to a quiet rest. I call on you to stop this now, if you have any respect at all. Are we black, proud, and Socialists—or what are we. Now stop this nonsense. Don't carry this on any more. You're exciting your children.

All over and it's good. No, no sorrow that it's all over. I'm

225

glad it's over. Hurry. Hurry, my children. Hurry. All I—the hands of the enemy. Hurry, my children. Hurry. There are seniors out here that I'm concerned about. Hurry. I don't want any of my seniors to this mess. Only quickly, quickly, quickly, quickly, quickly. Let's just—Good knowing you.

No more pain, Al. No more pain, I said, Al. No more pain. Jim Cobb is laying on the airfield dead at this moment. [Applause.] Remember, the Oliver woman said she—she'd come over and kill me if her son wouldn't stop her. These, these are the people—the peddlers of hate. All we're doing is laying down our lives. We're not letting them take our lives. We laying down our lives. Peace in their lives. They just want peace.

MAN: I'd like to say that my—my so-called parents are filled with so much hate and treachery. I think you people out here should think about your relatives were and be glad about that the children are being laid to rest. And I'd like to say that I thank dad for making me strong to stand with it all and make me ready for it. Thank you.

JONES: All they do is taking a drink. They take it to go to sleep. That's what death is, sleep.—I'm tired of it all.

WOMAN: Everything we could have ever done, most loving thing all of us could have done and it's been a pleasure walking with all of you in this revolutionary struggle. No other way I would rather go than to give my life for Socialism, Communism, and I thank Dad very, very much.

WOMAN: Dad's love and nursing, goodness and kindness and bring us to this land of freedom. His love—his mother was the advance—the advance guard to Socialism. And his love, his nurses will go on forever unto the fields of

JONES: to that, to that, to that, words to that—was the green scene thing.

WOMAN: Go on unto the sign. And thank you, Dad.

JONES: With the green—and please bring it here so the adults can begin.

—you don't, don't fail to follow my advice. You'll be sorry. You'll be sorry.

We do it, than that they do it. Have trust. You have to step across. We used to think this world was—this world was not our home, and it sure isn't—saying, it sure wasn't.

—don't want to tell them. All he's doing—if they will tell them—assure these—can't some people assure these children of the—in stepping over to the next plane. They set an example for others. We said— 1,000 people who said, we don't like the way the world is.

Take our life from us. We laid it down, we got tired. We didn't commit suicide, we committed an act of revolutionary suicide protesting the conditions of an inhumane world. [Organ music.]

Bibliographical Note

I HAVE USED, BEYOND sources noted in the text, the accounts of Jonestown and the aftermath published in the *New York Times* and the *San Francisco Chronicle*. I have also used materials graciously provided by the publicity office of the Disciples of Christ, and I wish to express public gratitude to Robert Friedly of that office for unfailing cooperation. The paperbacks put out by the *Washington Post (Guyana Massacre)* and the *San Francisco Chronicle (Suicide Cult)* were helpful both for some of the "evidence" they noted and for an insight into the direct and differing reactions of journalists on the scene. Charles Krause, in particular, demonstrated a candor in reporting that I hope will not be overlooked merely because the pressures of journalism necessitated such a swift publication of his account. I believe that this is a place to recognize and applaud the work of several journalists who raised early, embarrassing and—sadly—ignored points about Jim Jones and his activities. Lester Kinsolving, admittedly a controversial and sometimes "baiting" writer, demonstrated rare courage in sticking to his guns as early as 1972. There is some evidence, if the testimony of Terri Buford is to be credited, that Kinsolving risked considerably in stating his views. I believe his courage merits a retroactive recognition of sorts. Carolyn Pickering of the *Indianapolis Star* is another who merits commendation for early efforts. Ken Woodward of *Newsweek* deserves another such commendation for having

228

detailed most of the basic pre-Jonestown allegations more than a year before the end. Had his article not appeared in August, when churches go on vacation, it is hard to believe that a greater outcry would not have been heard.

Although I have had access to some basic documents—several of which are in the Appendixes—I have no doubt that there is a plethora of pertinent material yet unpublished. Some material on People's Temple was pilfered on the spot in Jonestown by journalists in search of exclusive angles. At some point it behooves someone to finance the collection in one place of as much pertinent documentation as can be found, if only because I believe a closer history needs to be written than is possible in a book such as this. The saga of Jim Jones is a rare instance in which the phenomenon of charismatic religion in the twentieth century has been other than "conservative." As I have tried to suggest, the phenomenon needs to be studied as an effort to achieve social goals via religious stratagems.

I see no need to list again works cited in footnotes. Some—by Lacan, Buber, Alvarez, Maritain, Schweitzer, and Haley—could be read in toto in order to get a deeper exposure to points I have tried to make. The Alvarez book is particularly important.

There are a number of works that I have consulted but that I have not noted (save for that of Lacan). These fall under the heading "structuralism," an intellectual school of which Claude Levi-Strauss and Michel Foucault are also members. Generally—because I am iconoclastic toward any intellectual effort that claims to be comprehensive—I do not have the same problem with structuralists as those critics who claim they are seeking the ultimate explanation of everything. All humanistic and scientific work seems to me finite. Nevertheless, a commitment to holistic thought leads one toward those who are willing to venture into various forms of "pattern thinking." I am drawn to what I understand of Foucault's archaeological approach to historical data and to his ideas on power, discourse, and the history of sexuality.

Gregory Bateson is another person of importance in the effort to move toward new thought patterns. Stewart Brand's *Co-Evolution Quarterly* seems to me a publication of some importance to those interested in ecological perspectives.

Authors who can be read with profit by those seeking both responsible analysis and some move beyond the constriction of disciplines are Robert Nisbet, Alice Rossi, Kate Millet, and Christopher Lasch—though I might wish to debate with the latter on the implications of his analysis of the family.

A general introduction to the present "state of the art" regarding group behavior, interpersonal relations, and manipulation is *Interpersonal Dynamics: Essays and Readings on Human Interaction*, edited by Warren Bennis, Edgar Schein, Fred Steel, and David Berlew. Schein's chapter on brainwashing is particularly pertinent.

Certain books get down to the nitty-gritty of social action, and the one I would most recommend—not without some criticism—is the late Saul Alinsky's *Rules for Radicals*.

The story of Father Divine is interesting enough; my bibliographical confession will doubtless seem an equally tall tale. Some years ago we stumbled on a paperback called *Father Divine: Holy Husband*. It was among the household books, and who knows how it got there? We read it avidly. It was beautifully written and a highly revealing examination of the structures of racism in America. Will you believe that in the wake of Jonestown we found the book, but the cover was missing, including the names of both publisher and author. It turned out there were *two* authors. After several trips to the library I ascertained that the book was published in hardback by Doubleday in 1953 and that its authors were Sara Harris and Harriet Crittendon. After the book was completed I determined that the Harris-Crittendon opus had been reprinted under the title *Father Divine* in a revised and expanded edition. It is this latter version which I have not—under pressure of time—obtained and to which I would turn the reader's attention. (My page references, perversely, are to the paperback based on the 1953 edition, which I have not been able to trace bibliographically.)

Literature about the various cultic phenomena ranges from such gory accounts as Ed Sanders' *The Family* (which speaks not only of Charles Manson but also of a whole netherworld of California cults) to Ted Patrick's *Let Our Children Go*. Patrick's book is a frankly popular account of extra-legal efforts to "kidnap" and "deprogram" persons who have been in the various cults. But it raises substantive questions, legal and moral, about various contending freedoms—the freedom of parents versus the freedom of their "of age" children; whether or not persons who enter cults can be said to be deceived and thence under "harmful" domination; and whether the dogmatic deprogramming approach of Patrick (fighting fire with fire) is not in itself putting the whole issue into the realm of professional football rather than of religion. I have come to feel more and more that sensitive firsthand journalism may provide a needed key to the understanding and early warning of various movements. This, in my view, is a strong argument for the no-strings-attached subsidy of independent religious journals by religious institutions and charitable foundations. There is one easily available paperback, William Petersen's *Those Curious New Cults* (New Canaan: Pivot, 1975) that gives a thumbnail sketch of a large number of fringe groups and a hasty evangelical critique of same. Frederick Sontag's *Sun Myung Moon* I find somewhat odd. It has the appearance of a copious and objective examination, but there are many points at which Sontag seems to bend over backward to give Moon the benefit of the doubt. What is betrayed at such moments is

231

Sontag's evident attraction to aspects of Moon's stance with which I profoundly disagree. So I have an argument against the book, but it remains a creditable effort to get inside a cult.

Along with the need for a book that traces many unresolved aspects of Jonestown, there is clearly need for a thorough investigative report in book form on the cults.